D0969862

An Archaeology of Days

An Archaeology of Days

by

Vivian Shipley

Negative Capability Press
Mobile, Alabama

Copyright 2019, Vivian Shipley
All right reserved

Printed in the United States of America
FIRST EDITION, 2019

ISBN 987-0-942544-72-5
Library of Congress Control Number: 2018965356

Cover and interior design by Dr. Jack Bedell and Marley Stuart
Final Production Editing by Megan Cary
Author photograph by Dr. Wayne Chapman

The cover photo is of the barns that still stand on the Charles and
Minnie Taber Shipley's farm in Howe Valley, Hardin County,
Kentucky.

Requests for permission to reproduce material from this work
should be sent to the author or:

Dr. Sue Walker, Editor
Negative Capability Press
62 Ridgelawn Drive East
Mobile, Alabama, 36608

www.negativecapability press.org
facebook.com/negativecapabilitypress

For my sisters,

Mary Alice Shipley
and
Linda Ellen Shipley

and

my granddaughter

Chloe Vivian Jokl

Acknowledgments

Grateful acknowledgment is made to the editors of the journals in which these poems, often in earlier versions and with different titles, first appeared: *The American Voice*, *Abiko Quarterly*, *The Alembic*, *Alhambra Poetry Calendar*, *Another Chicago Magazine*, *The Briar Cliff Review*, *Caduceus: Poets at Yale Art Place*, *Centennial Review*, *Chachalaca Poetry Review*, *The Christian Science Monitor*, *Cold Mountain Review*, *Connecticut Muse*, *Connecticut River Review*, *Crosswinds*, *Defined Providence*, *Eclectic: The Literary and Art Magazine of State University of West Georgia*, *E: Emily Dickinson Award Anthology*, *The Evansville Review*, *Flyway*, *Forgotten Women*, *The Harpweaver*, *The Hartford Courant*, *Heart*, *Heliotrope: A Journal of Poetry*, *Interim*, *The Journal*, *The Ledge*, *The Lowell Pearl*, *Louisiana Literature*, *The MacGuffin*, *Mississippi Review*, *Nebo*, *Negative Capability*, *New Letters*, *New Millennium*, *New Orleans Review*, *New York Quarterly*, *The New York Times*, *Nimrod*, *Paddlefish*, *Passages North*, *Paterson Literary Review*, *Pleiades*, *Poems and Plays*, *Poet Lore*, *Poets On*, *Prairie Schooner*, *Quarterly West*, *River Styx*, *San Diego Literary Review*, *San Pedro River Review*, *Shawangunk Review*, *Slant*, *So to Speak*, *The South Carolina Review*, *Sundog: The Southeast Review*, *The Texas Review*, *Two Rivers Review*, *Unlocking the Word: An Anthology of Found Poetry*, *The Vanderbilt Review*, *Whiskey Island Magazine*, *Wind*, *Yale Anglers Journal* and *Yemassee*.

Other Books by Vivian Shipley

Poems out of Harlan County (1989)
Devil's Lane (1996)
Crazy Quilt (1999)
Fair Haven (2000)
When There Is No Shore (2002)
Gleanings: Old Poems, New Poems (2003)
Hardboot: Poems New & Old (2005)
All of Your Messages Have Been Erased (2010)
The Poet (2015)
Perennial (2015)

Chapbooks

Jack Tales (1982)
How Many Stones? (1998)
Echo & Anger, Still (1999)
Down of Hawk (2001)
Fishing Poems (2001)
Greatest Hits: 1974-2010 (2011)

CONTENTS

I

CARGO

A plover with a broken wing flops
on the granite outcropping abutting
my seawall. At my computer, I cannot
avoid seeing it if I look out the window.

I can fold the newspaper on slaughters
in Syria, Myanmar, faces of children who can
no longer recognize their unveiled mothers
blown into concrete barricades or wedged under

car tires. To erase this bird, I must lose
my view of Long Island Sound, my beach.
The bird hops, stumbles dragging feathers.
Closing my blind, I blot out not only glare

but thought of the plover like the truck driver
in Laredo, South Texas who slammed rear doors
of his 18 wheeler on 73 illegal immigrants who
had crossed the Rio Grande by raft to stash houses.

Late July, 2017, the trucker knew air conditioning
did not work and the four vents were blocked.
On the interstate, sun-flash of semis, the cab cool,
in the back air was stale as a kiln, motion baked

out of it. The "King of Country," George Strait's
All My Exes Live in Texas on the radio drowned
heels of hands pounding like ball-peen hammers
on the metal wall. No way to torch the doors open.

Stopping at Walmart in San Antonio to relieve
himself, the driver opened trailer doors to pitch

black. Clobbered by light, bodies were birds that
scattered like a pack of cards thrown up into air.

One man lurched out, ran to a customer to beg
for water. Too late to shut doors, the trucker feigned
surprise at the cargo. Ten people dead, those too weak
to stand, did not leave. I open the blind, my bird

is gone. Then, like the human tide from Mexico,
back over the wall of rock it comes. I can block out
the sight, but now like the trucker, I can't ignore
its wing. What if the plover won't go away to die?

I'd like to believe I have a heart unlike the driver who
closed that trailer tractor door. Drawn by the bird's cries,
my dog leaps, straining to get on the beach. Knowing
what he will do, I'm tempted. Should I open the gate?

CONFESS: GLUTTONY

If design govern
   —Robert Frost

Clouds washboard sky. No pelican gliding,
neck folded back, it's a cormorant thrashing

the line of horizon like a wooden lawn ornament.
I know nicknames: water turkey, crow, and shark.

Landing on rocks below our seawall, head oiled
like a tango dancer, the bird spread-eagles to Dracula,

could be Shakespeare's *cormorant devouring Time*
in *Love's Labour's Lost.* Its neck and head are visible

like a submarine with periscope raised. Keeping the fish
population down, insatiate as famine, fire, or cancer, bill

up it could be a loon. Tailgating, catching fish crosswise,
I time the cormorant as it stays under more than a minute.

Diving over and over, never surfacing at the same point,
I wonder if it's looking for something lost, say, innocence?

I need to believe everything is a part of some plan.
The day is clear. I see Long Island's low, long mound

across the Sound. From where I stand in Connecticut, I
can't see the Atlantic's shore where black, slick heads

of divers, descended like the cormorant, again, again,
yet again through lashing surf. It's four years to the day.

July 17, 1996. The news from kickers in a trunk blared
from a car pulling into Wawa's: taking off for Paris

from Kennedy airport, TWA's Flight 800 exploded. All
230 people were killed. As if God could not leave earth

alone, a yellow mouth opened in the sky. No white trail
bisecting night glowed over the beach like fireworks.

No time to bury hands in faces, pillow against the seat
in front. For bodies kidnapped with no ransom, no time

for barnacles, only brine soaked clothing, profanity
of arms, legs, hands pulsating as if the ocean floor

was gagging on too much flesh. Searching for reason,
finding the black box was a prayer answered. Divers

pulled the plane up piece by piece. Parts were hauled
into a hangar like trash cans being pulled to the curb.

Unlike snappers and eels the cormorant I watch brings up
in its beak to swallow alive, no one on Flight 800 drowned.

No way to have conversation with a cormorant anymore
than God, than the 230 dead. Still, I cannot resist trying

any more than I can praying. I want to ask this cormorant
I watch each day at Morgan Point, do you feel remorse,

are you gnawed by demons that cause you to plunge, rise,
plunge, rise, as if damned by the hand of God? Descending,

do you have the urge to come upward to air, smelling
your way to rock where you were born like the father

who comes each year to where Flight 800 went down?
He is the anniversary marker for his daughter's death.

If the cormorant does not forget the last fish while beaking
the next fish, the burden of knowing hunger that will never

be filled must core it as grief does the father who jabs starfish
in low runnels of the Atlantic's surf. Chenille bodies grab

at his stick, just as he does for some answer from the ocean
that gives him nothing more than the cormorant I question.

His history, his future is his daughter's soccer ball on a table
and the bedroom ceiling she had strung with stars. His reason:

There is no sunrise each day. I try, but I can't let her go.
Headlines ecstatic in the mystery, the static, the static,

the blast but no solution for the explosion. Four years later,
no bomb, no heat seeking missile, no malfunction, no buildup

of electricity in Boeing 747 fuel tanks. All that breath will
never jet the Atlantic, rustle grass at Calais, fog to clouds

in the Alps, will never sweeten air for a mother who comes
to sit on the Long Island shore. Face trenched, she watches

for the sun to rise, to melt her grief as it does late snow.
She cannot hammer her days into an urn; while it ebbs,

water sucking reminds her of lips at her breast. Insatiate as
the cormorant, her son, a phantom limb toeing the side of

her stomach, is relentless, is the only interruption in a world
she waits out. No reason from TWA, no word from God,

it is an air current, not movement of angel wings she feels.
No keel is scraping, only sand no hourglass can contain.

NATURE, RED IN TOOTH AND CLAW

In Memoriam
    —Alfred Lord Tennyson

For the life of me, I can't fathom why my son
spends hours floating by a breakwater protecting
New Haven's harbor from Long Island Sound.
Trailing an eel or sand worm, Todd crams

his six feet, five inches into an orange kayak,
only to catch and release. If he were sensible,
thrifty like me, he'd utilize his time, stock up
on filets from blues or stripers. How can he fish

not for the flesh but for the solitude, to nourish his
spirit? Tonight, it may have been a return
to childhood need to impress his father and me
that prompted him to bring back a striped bass

over forty inches long. Watching Todd hoist it like
bagged top soil for my camera, I figure—fifty
pounds. Calling the fish, *she*—it was too fat to be a
male—my son tries to return life he's taken

back into the water. All elbows, wading by touch in
the pewter cove, slow dancing with the striper,
Todd holds her tail for well over a half an hour.
Because mosquitoes are biting his neck, I resist

saying the fish will end up a floater a day later.
Responding to my silent cheerleading on our deck,
she does not swim. I'd learned to rationalize death
of what I eat in a Siem Reap market while watching

a Buddhist Cambodian woman who would not kill
in order to eat flesh. Admiring fish just hauled out
of Tonle Sap, a large freshwater lake anchoring
the town's southerly tip, she said a carp would be

perfect for a curry. Her mouth covered by one hand,
she mumbled it was too bad the fish was still alive.
The fishmonger caught up to her as she paused
at another stall, shouting out the miracle—the carp

had suddenly died! Having given up on a resurrection
in the cove, my son appears to tease the striped bass
back to life separating skin with his knife, slicing
from behind the gill plate to the bottom of the spine.

Curious about what it's eaten, plunging into the guts,
Todd pulls out a whole lobster then another claw.
To show off my Victorian PhD, I give my son a quick
course on Darwin's *Origin of Species*. Even though

I know what he will find, I quote from *In Memoriam:*
*we trust that somehow good / Will be the final goal
of ill.* Blood slicking forearms, his hand probing, Todd
will feel how firmly the heart roots before it gives way.

TRESPASSERS AT MORGAN POINT

Cautious as a stag leading does in a clearing, two fishermen look
    toward the house, just checking. As if crossing a lawn they'd
newly seeded, their steps are shortened, rods held low.

Heading for black rocks, one holds a hand of his son, knowing
    full well their Zodiac is beached above high water on pink
granite. Not trying to claim they're lost, confused, sorry,

it's anger that simmers in throats, idling like an outboard motor
    as I point to *Private Property*. A United jet taking off from
Tweed New Haven censors, *bitch*. No Roger Peterson,

the two won't teach the boy to tell snowy egret from white heron
    by an egret's black bill, legs and yellow feet. Busy popping caps
off Budweiser, the father doesn't see another egret

shuffling feet about to stir up shiners, a habit white herons
    don't have. Teaching his son to break bottles for fun,
he calls a cormorant *crow* as it spreads wings. We are all

trespassers of one sort or other but that does it! I dial East Haven
    police, demand protection. Then, I gloat while snapper after
snapper jumps drawn by a magnet in the cove. Badge

or no badge, the two fishermen will resurface, boy along to carry
    beer. Good or bad days, they'll be back. If rip tide feathers
the Sound, it will be a sign to them, irrepressible as tide.

THE DODO

March madness, basketball, finished, T.S. Eliot
had it right, *April is the cruelest month*. Not one
for *mixing/Memory and desire, stirring/Dull roots
with spring rain,* my Mondays are for full strength

bleach, the wash. Tuesdays are for steeping bags I
use for cold tea. Wednesdays, I go to book signings;
yesterday was New Haven, Yale University Press.
I must have been two sandwiches short of a picnic

when I lined up to get Beverly and Stephen Stearns
to autograph a copy of *Watching, From the Edge
of Extinction* for my father. From their first sentence,
I know right where his mind is heading. Off Africa's

southeast coast are the volcanic Mascarene, dubbed
islands of the living dead because species have adapted
to life without predators and disease, just like my father
who refused yearly physicals, ignored prostate cancer.

Mauritius, the Mascarene home of the dodo, has
the world's only known *Hyophorbe amaricaulis.*
The minute this palm gets blown over on the cyclone
prone island, that's the end. That's it. My father starts

up: he's the last of his line. Both his brothers buried,
their children are all *dad blamed girls*, nary a boy
in the whole bunch. When he dies, his name will be
dead as a dodo. Who will remember Uncle Justus

who had devils dancing in green eyes, Aunt Laverne
who was too pure for this earth, Uncle Paul blowing

his nose so loud at the Methodist revival, he had to
apologize to the preacher? Their names are in me,

a jumble in the Sunday comics, no one can unscramble.
Not the sharpest knife in the drawer, I flip to another
chapter. Researchers now take notes, snap photos
as an organism's fate becomes sealed, the necrology

to record the moment when, teetering on the brink,
a species begins the irreversible descent into the abyss.
Those last hopeless days of *Hyophorbe amaricaulis*
will not go unrecorded. I don't have sense enough

to put wire over the top of a chimney to keep wolves
from coming down. How on earth will I explain Brandy,
a student I have hired to videotape my father's stories?
No lollygagging, set in my ways, one to finish what

I start, sop the last bit of gravy, I plunge right on
to the end of *Watching, From the Edge of Extinction*.
My luck changes: there's a revival of the living dead,
the Mauritius Kestrel. Once the rarest falcon in the world,

down to a few pairs, after thirty years of captive breeding
and release, there are hundreds of Mauritius Kestrels.
Always heading into the day after tomorrow, I remind
my father he's like a bat who has the hang of dodging

objects, how the love he will leave behind is more lasting
than a name, will stay, stuck like the bones, the quills
of a porcupine he shot in our hickory tree. A girl who
wants to be a substitute of sorts, a boy, I cannot pull

my father's skeleton through me. I can give him dandelion
wine, lard crusts, fireflies in mason jars, build a fluttermill

by Rough Creek, fly a Mauritius Kestrel to heaven. Tailed like a kite, it will go ahead to see what my father will see.

SOURDOUGH

I just know I can be a good role model.
Nothing can be as bad as the bully
in 7th grade—not even this—having

my sourdough starter die. Resilient,
I will not let it become a metaphor,
a setback, sure, a part of the journey,

but not a career ending failure. In fact,
with sourdough, I had deliberately invited
tension into my life, believing as a human,

I needed stress as much as bread. Kneading
it, I take breaks like I do in weight lifting reps.
A bit of fermented flour, a microbial jumble

of bacteria and yeast, sourdough not only
is uplifting but also gives anything baked
a complex tang. No philodendron I can

forget to water or a low maintenance
goldfish, sourdough's health is a reflection
of my maturity, ability to take responsibility.

My dead starter could have been from, say,
a rare bloom of mold, too much time
forgotten on the kitchen counter in August—

or what I feared—lethargy, neglect pure
and simple neglect on my part. I see
the starter's death as a chance to rethink

my life goals and find what truly fulfills
my spirit, not just my stomach. I swear
sourdough's demise will not be in vain!

It will inspire me to get out of my comfort
zone—maybe not climb Mount Kilimanjaro
or run a triathlon, but I might share my secret

poetry journal at a slam. I will be an optimist.
Sourdough starters are sturdy, can live long
untragic lives passed from mother to child

to child and back again. Why, I know one
in Brooklyn that celebrated a 60th birthday!
I'll get a packet of dry sourdough starter,

mix it up, feed once a week with flour, milk,
let ferment overnight—but I will not fail to
think ahead. Forget to reserve some airy mass

for next week and my high hopes might vanish.
There will not be another batch of pancakes
as thick and even as a layer of birthday cake

to anticipate. I'll even give a part of my starter
to everyone I know. Share don't hoard will
be my motto—it ensures survival. If I make

rolls, dust with cinnamon sugar, no matter
what happens between today, and the days
ahead, something sweet will be waiting.

Open, Sesame

My birthday dinner, I've given up stilettoes,
even Manolo Blahnik's Amiela shoe,
its elongated pointy toe, rounded tip
like the beak of a swan, spindly heel flaring

at the base to resemble how my champagne
flute's stem widens as if to blow bubbles.
Last to go were Manolo's brick shoes,
heels of cork covered with black patent leather,

green inserts for my feet, toenails scarlet letters.
Yet, I persist in believing I am still decadent
like the sesame seeds I pick at on my roll—
think how much pure life is in each one!

Deep and intense as existence itself,
1.2 million different kinds of seeds are like
the caviar before me, glossy fish eggs
containing the entire organism of their origin.

Why in *Ali Baba and the Forty Thieves,*
the command to a seedpod, *Open Sesame,*
unlocks a treasure cave. I know Greek myth
blames winter on Persephone for eating

pomegranate seeds in Hades, but pomegranate
seeds, by legend, number 613 and in Jewish
midrash, *The Just* eat each of them to fulfill
the 613 good deeds ordered by God's oldest law.

Once I hit 70, it was hard to stop thoughts from
being morbid: when crops failed, the last thing

humans ate were seeds. In the Great Famine
of 1315-1317, thousands of English, French

and Germans starved even after freeze and flood
passed because grain seed had all been eaten.
During Ireland's potato famine, an 1847 harvest
was blight-free but produced only a fourth

of what was needed because most seed potatoes
had been eaten in the previous wretched spring.
Just a year shy of 75, it's high time I examine
my moral fiber, character. Would I have been

like brave Russian scientists in 1934, inspired
not by patriotism but by their leader Vavilov
who had collected the seeds himself? They all
starved to death in a St. Petersburg vault

with the world's largest seed collection rather
than allow the hordes to eat them. Or, reaching
for more butter, would I ask like the Roman stoic,
Seneca the Younger, *When shall we live if not now?*

Portal 31, Harlan County, Kentucky

To inhale odorless whiff of danger, of death, tourists like me
have unzipped Lynch's Main Street to visit the mine tunneled
miles beneath Black Mountain in 1917 by U.S. Coal and Coke.
Statistics impress me: for 40 years, one million tons of coal
per year was shouldered through Portal 31; loading coal onto
rail cars, Lynch's tipple was the largest in the world. First stop

is the bath house with pictures of men surfacing on Saturday
to soak out earth they burrowed in all week. A fan of reality
TV shows, I take my turn at a pump handle, prime with water
from a jug by the well. Rising from a coffin shaped tub,
wrapped in white towels, men flapped arms to angel wings—
as close to heaven as miners could get. For one day, what

they drew from the earth cleansed them. The mine entrance
stops me like a sentinel. Peering inside isn't enough; I want
the real thing—not actual miles burying miners but to bore
800 feet back—short level walk out if our man-rail car comes
off track. Sure enough, Junior Owens who will be my guide
worked this shaft with my kin. I'll bet he figures I'm another

Yankee tourist because I'm sporting Gucci sunglasses, posing
for selfies by granite memorials for John L. Lewis and miners
who were killed in Lynch. Pointing out the stone paver near
Portal 31 with my cousin's name, I ask Junior if he remembers
Jack Taber who always worked the extra shift to *lead the sheet*
by loading the most tons in a week. Jack would tell anyone in

earshot how on February 12, 1923, he helped set a world record
for a 9 hour shift when miners operating 40 shortwall cutting
machines produced 12,820 tons of coal, filling 256 railcars.
Getting back to my Kentucky roots, I've already figured out

how I can help out at Portal 31: open an upscale gift shop
with licorice bits of candy coal in tin lunch buckets, blue jeans

by Versace with ripped knees and blackened handprints.
Certain a PR guy that wrote about safety for the web site never
dipped a toe in *bug dust*, ground coal left by cutting machines,
I'm not stepping a foot inside unless we stay in the sturdiest part.
I'd read about the May 20, 2006 blast at Darby Mine No. 1
in Holmes Mill, Kentucky—five miners buried in falling debris,

one got out. With no need for a paycheck each week to feed
my family, I can insist on tunnel walls coated to bind coal;
double the number of four foot bolts to hold overhead rock;
unused mine tunnels sealed to keep out methane. Loaded into
a taxi yellow car with an overhead metal cab—a belt, safety pin
and suspender woman—I sit next to a man who's strong enough

to carry me out. Overhead, a voice warns, *Keep arms and legs*
inside. Remember safety first—it's our motto at Portal 31.
Always has been. Recorded laughter and singing from miners
going underground is even harder for me to swallow. A canary
punctuating black signals first stop, 1919: an animatronic miner,
Joseph Marzelli, says in a heavy accent I label Italian, *As long*

as I can hear your song, I know I'm safe. Flanked by his mule,
he points out its harness weighted with picks, shovels, dynamite.
A Welshman, one of 38 nationalities in Lynch, yells, *Fire in the*
hole. Then rumble, an explosion that startles Marzelli's mule,
who calms him, *Easy, calmare, Aren't you used to that noise?*
Waving us on with *Life is bellissimo,* water drips from the roof—

the only thing that's real. I might as well be watching Mickey
Mouse at Disney World. Another stop: a miner with head bowed
by a 6-foot ceiling loads coal onto a car for another man to haul.
Robots, they squat, kneel, stoop or crawl. Human, a body wasn't

made to move that way. Pausing, metal heads swivel to mouth
WWII, grateful they weren't like cousins in Cincinnati whose

women worked at Proctor and Gamble, who didn't have biscuit
and gravy waiting for them. It was 1941. Baseball got miners
through 14 hour shifts: Ted Williams batted .406, Joe DiMaggio
hit safely in 56 games, 42-year-old Lefty Grove had his 300th
win. Then Pearl Harbor: Ted Williams, Marine flight instructor;
Jolting Joe, Army Sergeant. Navy fielded: Pee wee Reese,

second baseman, Phil Rizzuto, shortstop, Johnny Mize, first
basemen. No more time for talk of life above ground, moving on,
we watch an inspector check air quality. Finally, Junior Owens
does come clean, reveals there was no protection from black
lung, how a newcomer was marked by the way he covered
his nose and mouth. I ask Junior where Sago Mine inspectors

were in West Virginia when 12 miners died January 2, 2006.
At least four air packs didn't work. Men shared oxygen masks
like chicken at Sunday supper when there was never enough
to go around. Junior's got no time for an answer. Next exhibit:
robots drilling into walls of coal. Bodies vibrating drown out
their voices, slices of life miners lived on earth: shooting craps

by Looney Creek on Sundays, sudden rain that changed its dry
bed of rocks to a riffle of sepia and long trails of roped bark.
I want to hear about wives whose hearts were seeded with worry
of husbands in a coffin, thin wash of rouge on cheeks to cover
a life lived underground. Surely, sorrow didn't stop summer,
laughter like firecrackers after dark, or spring moonlight limning

a woman, her man as she unbound her hair on Black Mountain.
No time for wonder, our man-rail cart jerks us to the next stop:
a machine that's a machine with teeth to chew coal from black
veins of the Appalachians. Modern, a continuous mining exhibit

doesn't show a conveyor rumbling to life with no warning,
gnawing off the left arm above the elbow of a preacher. Let go

by the mine, he could still shout, lift up a Bible in his right hand
at the pulpit of Free Pentecostal Church. To give back hope
to disabled veterans returning from WWII, he preached about
Pete Gray who played for the St. Louis Browns from April
to September, 1945. He was inspired by Pete, also from a mining
town of Nanticoke, Pennsylvania, who was the only one-armed

man ever to play major league baseball. Falling from a wagon
at 12, losing his arm to wheel spokes, Pete never questioned
God's plan, learned to bunt, planting the bat's knob against
his side, then sliding his hand a third of the way up the shaft.
Opposing pitchers saw he couldn't hit breaking pitches, threw
curve balls but Pete still batted in 13 runs. His career ended

on V-J Day when baseball stars returned from the battlefront.
Our eighth and final stop, multiple video images are projected
on rock surfaces. Now, I had hoped end of the line would be
a room with projectors reeling an Oscar winning film, *Harlan
County, USA*, about a 1974 strike. For perspective, I'd add music
of two fingered banjo pickers named Skillet Lickers, Fruit Jar

Drinkers, Possum Brothers playing for square dancing called
by Stringbean, Little Jimmy Dickens, Grandpa Jones. Go right,
go left, *break* into fours: duck for the oyster, shoot the buffalo.
In a grand finale at a 13th century copper mine in Falun, Sweden,
I'd paid for gunshots to echo. Junior says: *No!* There are last
words, voices of his brother, father, he doesn't want to awaken.

Jai Alai in Connecticut

A fan in the highest bleachers
of Bridgeport's fronton,
you cannot see
the color of my eyes
but they are not green or blue.

I will not salute
to you from mid court
as a sign of respect
by raising up the cesta
tied to my wrist.

When you lose, you curse
in English ever I understand,
would spit in my face
if you could get near me
as you rip up the betting
slips printed with my name
you don't try to pronounce.

HOW MUCH TIME HE GAINS WHO DOES NOT LOOK TO SEE WHAT HIS NEIGHBOR SAYS OR DOES

Meditations
   —Marcus Aurelius

Sunflowers are promiscuous, don't respect borders,
even ones ordered by a president, migrate Mexico
to Texas. Burrowing willy-nilly, they encourage
cross-fertilization, actually thrive on energy from

the African diaspora. A sunflower's life is full
of aggravations: rust beetles, moths, bears rolling
in them for fun, midges, weevils, and blackbirds.
Thoughtful refugees, sunflowers need little fertilizer

and don't need irrigation. Resettling, they scavenge
nutrients left in soil by natives who cultivate grains
like wheat or rye. Given a chance, sunflower roots
can go down 8 feet, renewing a new neighbor's soil.

A heritage of their own, archaeologists found seed
caches in Tennessee dating from 3000 B.C. Binding
the globe, they don't stick to a species: cardinals
and grosbeaks crack the hull of seeds and little birds,

chickadees and goldfinches, prefer hulled seeds.
A cultural barometer, Spanish like the recreation
of crack-and-spits but Japanese label sunflowers
in shells as bird food—give them one and they

will not spit it out. A Russian can outdo everyone
with a Khrushchev shoe pounding approach, cracking
a steady stream of seeds on one side of the mouth
dislodging kernels with his tongue and spitting hulls

from the other. The French think crack and spits are
as uncivilized as eating corn on the cob. No need to
build walls, sunflowers are a taste all share. Never
cranky but happy multiculturalists, no rift or rupture

over color—on the reservation, Hopi women made
purple dye from seeds. Like Hidatsa, *people of the
willow*, living only in North Dakota, humans are tribal
but sunflowers show how porous boundaries can be.

Foxwoods Casino at Ledyard

Chase the ivory ball across the wheel.
18 to 38—red or black, odd or even,
2—38—0 or 00;
2 to 38—1st, 2nd or 3rd 12;
1 to 36—any number.

Breath in.
Drop 4 quarter chips
on the black, 2 nickels on 13,
4 nickels on 00.

Pray to win. Lose, you
can begin to repay the Pequots
with arrowheads and spears
plowed up on your father's farm
in Howe Valley outside Cecelia
that you boxed in Kentucky
and carried with you to Connecticut.

On the 33rd Floor of the Hyatt

Overlooking San Diego's harbor,
looking down from my window
into a courtyard of what might

have once been a mission, I watch
a man hose off a chestnut brown horse
with a dramatic Mae West mane.

The horse's ribs are not distinct.
Washing everywhere, he even lifts
its tail. I think it must be very beautiful

for the man to spend so much time; it's
how he shows love. A sombrero hides
his face. After brushing to remove water,

he leaves the horse tethered to chain link
without a pat or a scratch behind the ear.
Nothing to drink, no food, no shade,

the horse can't move except to step left,
then right. Far above this man, he would
not hear me if I spoke but I'd like to tell

him my rescue pit bull, Goldie, sleeps
on down cushions. Afraid of confrontation,
I won't descend in the elevator to protest.

A sign on his building offers scenic tours.
To this man, I suppose an animal is just
an animal he uses to harness for a carriage.

No need to waste an apple, he pulls one
from his pocket, polishes it on his vest
only at the end of the ride to coax tips

from overweight tourists like me. If I
didn't have to get up from my chair to
get the phone, I would call the concierge.

Searching for Breakfast

Cornell Art Museum, Florida
   —Elfreda Shragen

Why do three chickens pecking under palm trees
in this painting unearth a straitjacket for me? Flat,
folded, sleeves open and reach out like white wings
flapping the backyard my father fenced trying to be
Grandpa who never reined in chickens that ran wild,
nested in his Hardin County barns, laid eggs in hay.

Never a one-sided chase, did the cackle, the flutter,
attempt to flee cast iron pan whet Daddy's appetite?
No Crayola's, he learned colors the hard way: blue
from gizzards; green, a gall bladder's bile; red was full
blown roses blossoming in water bucketing away
blood. He wouldn't answer when I asked if he palmed

nubbin of heart, blew to inflate lungs that held no more
breath than his pouch of aggies, sucked and released
along with the esophagus as it was pulled down through
the neck. My father insisted on ordering our chickens
from a Kentucky farm but not one like Grandpa's.
These were bred just for slaughter. Raised in crates

after hatching, packed for shipping standing up wing
to wing, Daddy's batch of fryers were too weak to walk.
The optimist, each morning before his coffee, he
lifted them from the chicken house he had built,
positioned them, statues on the grass of three roosters
and fifteen hens that had been cooped up too long.

It should have been easy for him to wring their necks.
Pecking at corn, they would have given up without

a struggle, refusing to scatter. Was it boyhood need
for thrill of the chase that left him unable to kill or did
my father expect chickens to be Syrian suicide bombers,
twist off their heads, plaster ground with their own blood?

Mango Season in Cambodia

Tired of annotating my scars, trying to gain perspective
about my ordinary deaths, I watch men who have given

both legs to land-mines scoot on wheeled wooden sleds
to beg in the center of town or on the apron of a road.

Not wanting to founder in grief, I avoid lure of *stupas,*
burial monuments like one I just bought for my parents.

Trees fringing field scrub are deep violet in predawn
and remind me of my mother's inner elbows when blood

was taken or bruises on my father after early morning falls.
Nothing has ever scoured me like grief of women

who saw daughters dissolve on Pol Pot's forced marches
north into the jungle, or were forced to witness husbands

being eviscerated for *sin of greed* after eating foraged yams.
Sent to herd cattle, clear land, build huts, hearts that lived

through Khmer Rouge ruptured at the suicide of sons
who could not endure the crawl of that world. Ache

left in those mothers that nothing will soothe helps me
right myself. I'd vowed not to try and escape my loss

on tour buses that chase sunrise to ruins at Angkor Wat,
but learn from Cambodian food branded by the grief

of Khmer cooks who parse sweet and sour notes, alternate
solid and liquid, raw and boiled. As I take in bitter heat

from herbs and wild greens, sourness of lemongrass
opposed to that of tamarind, I can taste chicory my mother

taught me to grind for coffee, dandelion I picked for salad.
Tonguing young pineapple, lime vinegar, green mango

and papaya, I remember sour mash fermenting to sweetness
whiskey can bring. Understanding my hunger, a chef

in Siem Reap explains that memory of curried fish laced
with bamboo and water lilies nourishes his spirit, thought

of pork stewed in caramelized palm sugar sustains him,
but trying to regain one perfect meal, one perfect taste

he had created was as futile as trying to bring back
my parents. Still I am on edge, watch a street vendor

make a shallow incision in a mango and pull upward,
lifting rather than slicing blushing skin. Even sound

of the green peel ripping away is unsettling. To soothe
myself, I accept his offer to sample three kinds. Flesh

of the cheapest and most common is gaudy orange,
fibrous and cloyingly sweet. His mid-range mango,

the dusty orange gold of monks' robes, is also sweet,
but slivers of sour run through it, like ice. Treating

myself to his most expensive mango, I let juice drip
down my chin. Sweetness is balanced by spicy, musky,

and tart flavors. Flesh is smooth and creamy, the color
of the gold moon or forsythia my mother forced to bloom

by putting brown sugar in a vase. I had not traveled
to Cambodia for the mango season, but biting into fruit,

I found what I was seeking—how it is bitterness which
eventually numbs the tongue and sourness which lingers

in the mouth that changes the way things taste, and how
the sweet becomes sweeter next to sorrow, next to grief.

Sister

I. At Night, Paula Hitler
Thinks of Her Brother

No one to chase, but like a dog chained
to a tree, how quickly the heart gets entangled,

how impossible for it to go back. Tethered
to my brother by bone, by DNA, I would

chew loose if I could, or take up clubs to settle
our differences if I lived in another time.

Unwind, and I can poke my finger through
metal webs of the porch glider I crawled under

to hiss and make my brother think: *snake.*
My back was to the concrete. Adolph jumped.

I laughed. We were not old; he did not use
my first communion photo as coaster for coffee.

In Linz, we laid under the yellow plum tree
by our side yard. Waiting for fruit to drop

into open mouths, we turned over, over again.
Grass greened our knees, but did not leave

a stain like my love for my brother does,
blood red, a candle dripping in my heart.

II. Paula Hitler, Ice Skating with
Her Brother in the Waldviertel

Blades picking ice, I barreled,
but you would dip first one shoulder then
the other to the girls hooded in fur, linking
arms at the other end of the lake. I would
like to invent an afternoon for us like this:
in perfect parallel strides,
we would connect hands to form full
moons, or be Shakers in concentric circles,
arms spread wide to God. Adolph, how
unexpected it would have been, however
briefly, to be just once spinning in the
center of your attention. What I do
remember is this: us practicing edges,
pushing our weight left and right, cutting
crescents into wet ice already scarred, then
me tripping over divots you had made no
thaw could fill in or smooth over.

III. The Berghof: Paula Hitler Nurses
Her Brother Back to Health

Adolph, see how elm and beech mix
with firs, leaf to a dome that protects us.
Trees are scored with Nordic runes, twin

SS lightning bolts. I've come from Vienna
to Berchtesgaden to nurse you back to health.
Late March, even I know your war is not going

well. Only a persistent flu caused you to invite
me. I closed my eyes on the drive up on hairpin
turns to Obersalzberg. 1907, our mother died.

I was eleven, you were eighteen, and would
not watch her claw that left breast, as if
she could unnest the pain, the cancer. I did,

fingering her pearl and ivory rosary that you
tried to rip apart. Our mother, who taught us
to enunciate, to stare straight in another's eye,

would not like how you mutter as you walk
with a whip. Watching you slash off necks
of flowers you cannot name weights my chest;

I pick up green poppy heads that, like you, coil
their bloom in a snake's head. I can't swallow.
Sometimes my heart reaches out too far.

IV. The Heart

A brother I was born to, like the grave, Adolph,
you must have had a roadmap I did not get.
In interviews, I use *sibling*, avoid your name.
As a child, I chameleoned, never used *I* after one
of your lectures: *It's always about you, Paula.*
Be quiet. Listen to me when I speak. I tried,

but I didn't hear the word my heart needed.
I hung on to promises of afternoons together
for so long, they became beans our grandmother
left to dry on Spital's fences that rattled in wind,
in my heart. If I sleep, in dreams about you,
my brother, I cry out: *Bring me back to the Berghof,*

not Angela, our half-sister. Let me keep house
for you, cook for Mussolini, King Boris of Bulgaria,

brew the Duke of Windsor's tea. Put my picture
by your bed, not Geli's. Your niece spattered
her blood over your apartment walls, woke up
your neighbors on Munich's Prinzregentenplatz.

I would have been more considerate, never have
chosen your gun as a way to die. Years accordion,
but mostly they stick together. A few stand out:
Angela calling Eva Braun a *stupid goose* right
to her face; the two weeks I spent at the Berghof
nursing you back to health when you even recalled

how I came to visit you in the hospital after you
were gassed in 1918. I was the proudest sister
in Germany as you received the Iron Cross,
First Class. I still feel heat of late August when I
touch the picture of you, my corporal, my brother,
as I pretended to pin the medal on your jacket.

As usual, my tongue would not stay in my mouth
and I begged you to put your arm around me,
if only for the photographer, for the record.
Will my anger ever lift its weight from me,
a crescent moon rising over *Mein Kampf*
where you did not mention me, Paula Hitler,

even though you were writing it in your room
the day I was there? Words you did not say
will not release me, even when I am laid under
SISTER cut in stone. What is done cannot be
undone except by my heart which has no teeth
to chew, will not swallow what it cannot digest.

V. Berchtesgaden's Public Secret

That's what Florien Beierl calls me. Afraid,
I have signed a lease as Frau Wolf, but Adolph,
everyone knows I am your sister. Illegitimate,
our father, Alois, had our grandmother's name,
Shicklgruber. Because you used his surname,

Hitler, I did too. Before shooting yourself in Berlin,
you said farewell to Joseph Goebbels and Albert Speer,
but left no word for me. Adolph, why did you close
your heart, shape it into a fist that's become an incubus
pounding in my veins? To the end, Eva Braun,

common shop assistant, was cowardly, took poison.
How could you disgrace our family and, marry her
the day before you committed suicide? No concern
for my fate, your death was not an end stopped line.
I was left adrift, an outcast in two ground floor

rooms near the train station. New tenants upstairs
say it's strange that I do not take refuge in my alias,
lose myself in another town's festivals. I will not
tell them I take comfort being near what remains
of you. Early on in April, the SS abandoned

the Berghof. Neighbors, women I thought were friends,
went with or without wagons, carried what they could.
Not much is left of your house, Adolph, only door handles,
patio stones someone will soon have in their back yard.
My butcher allows me to lift the receiver of a phone

he yanked out of your bedroom, but the dentist who took
six volumes of your Shakespeare won't let me massage
the swastika or your initials, A.H., on leather spines.

I do not dare tell them I have the four letters you sent
me in 1924 from Landsberg sewn into my mattress.

That fat, swarthy woman who sells eggs denies me
even a snip of your hair, gotten, she says, from the barber
who brags each day that he trimmed the Fuhrer's mustache
even though he knows, as I finally do, how bodies
of children shriveled, how the ash lifted with the smoke,

rising slowly because it was heavy with bone. Yet,
I cannot corral our childhood by stopping memory
of you, my shield in the streets of Linz, or the bonfires
you lit each fall to amuse me. Adolph, stiff as a scarlet
taffeta skirt, my heart still cartwheels if I hear your name.

VI. *Please remember he was my brother.*
   —Paula Hitler

Brother, it is May 1945; you are dead. George Allen,
United States Army Intelligence, wants to question me.
He knows I am Paula Hitler. I refuse. I must go out

to the bakery. If I am late, dark brown rye will be gone.
The interpreter promises me bread; I have no excuse.
Adolph, shut up in a car with them, pressured to say

something about you, I try *die schonsten Zeiten meines
Lebens*, how you passed the most beautiful time
of your life in the Berghof's ramble of three stories,

balconies, and picture windows. Pitched roofs
intersected like a jigsaw puzzle of our life I never
solved. I hope detail satisfies George Allen: white

armchairs under striped umbrellas on a patio, Eva
holding Goebbels's little girl whose hair was topped
with a white satin bow shaped like the swastika

stitched onto a white patch on your left sleeve.
Finally, George Allen smiles, takes notes as I recall
how you never cared much for meat in our youth.

Our mother gave us cheese, fish, and game fowl,
but no blood sausage, veal, or roasted flesh. Even so,
you buttered toast as if flaying sinew from a bone.

Cheese ravioli would have been one of your final
meals. I picture you cleaning your plate while Eva
picked at the pasta as she lit cigarette after cigarette.

Indifferent to clothes and food, you never smoked,
drank tea, coffee, or alcohol. Hungry, hoping to free
myself from endless interrogation, get loaves of rye,

I uncover the scar, a new moon, your teeth left
on my left arm. No fermata of love, it is a lesson
I do not forget even for fresh bread. Our interpreter,

editing *lower-middle-class woman of great religion*
but no intelligence, does not realize I understand
English. He does translate that I'm a sister *whose*

misfortune it was to be related to a famous person
with whom she had nothing in common. Provoked,
I offer the men what is not mine to give: your tears

at our mother's death. How can this uniformed man
understand that blood we share still pulses in me
like your knee knocking, knocking at the underside

of our kitchen table? My heart has not uncoupled
from my mind, and to stop George Allen, I begin
to sob, show him what he wants so he will not need

the translator. At last, he concludes: *It is clear you have
been deeply affected by your brother's fate.*
I reply, frightened, *By his personal fate, of course.*

VII. Paula Hitler's Last Confession

Father Gustaf, you ask what it is I will not forgive.
My grievances against my brother that I cannot
dilute or dissolve, arrow my heart. Memory
is a wave carrying a log from the cove only to

wash it back in a storm. Does forgiveness come
in the telling of a story? If so, let me tell you mine.
Our father died. Adolph was fourteen and failing in
school to defy him. Hanging out with sculptors,

working with wood, he'd learned about the heart,
how it splits like timber down the full length
of the plank. Take a solid piece, drive in a wedge,
give a hard twist, and it will crack end to end. All

my brother needed to learn was where the grain lay.
Unlike our father who never spoke of love, showing
it in his will and life insurance he left, Adolph could
break my heart with a word. Mother's lapdog, clever,

systematic, for three years before her death, Adolph
withdrew small amounts from our father's trust so

51

the theft would not be noticed. And what could I do
once I knew what had been done—hire a lawyer?

No sum could replace what had been stolen. Dying
of cancer, our mother gathered up strength to sign
an undated lined yellow page giving my brother
an allowance to live in Vienna. Left with nothing,

I had to forage in Linz. How can I die in peace when
the words *treachery, theft, deceit, cunning* jackhammer
my heart? I suppose there was concern for my safety.
Before leaving, Adolph taught me how to break a finger

with my teeth—right below the knuckle is easier to grip.
Father, I confess I took pleasure when he was denied
entrance to the Academy of Fine Arts. Painting postcards
and advertisements, my brother shut me out by moving

from one Vienna room to another. Years passed, I sinned
again, cursed when Angela, not even a full sister, came
to live at the Berghof. Her daughter, Geli, killed herself
because of Adolph's jealousy. I spit *blood-kin* in his face,

held up their picture to goad him: Geli stretched beneath
his chair, the bold geometry of her sundress in contrast
to grass, her saddle shoes, white socks. I had never been
given such a look from him. Father, it does not matter

what history makes of me. Invent a life for the press—
I ate persimmons, roasted chestnuts. Report hope I had
for my brother's love still mocked me, a maraca luring
me onto the floor when there was no one left to dance.

VIII. Father Gustaf, Giving Last Rites to Paula Hitler

Unlike your brother who committed the ultimate sin
by taking his own life in Berlin, you will be buried
not burned. If you had been in his bunker, you would

have cried out, *Adolph, you never left the Church.*
Do not leave it now. Wait as I do; let God take you.
Let Him take you to our mother. Paula, you might

have persuaded Magda Goebbels not to take the lives
of her six children by forcing capsules of cyanide
into their mouths while they slept. Our townspeople

do not practice *Sippenhaft,* punishment for the crimes
of blood relations. At the gate of *Schonau am Konigsee,*
the cemetery director who understands a heart can crowd

out the mind will not admit those who come to desecrate,
only mourners to commemorate, to light a votive candle.
Paula, your brother's already our history. There's no way

to understand the absolute monster he was, to revise evil.
Your family is remembered. Dollensheim's square was
renamed *Alois Hitler Platz* after your father; Spital has

put wreaths on your mother's birthplace. The best I can
do is buy you a plain oak cross that will be protected
by a metal box sunk into the hillside of headstones.

The inscription will be: *PAULA HITLER:* 1896-1960.
Like a poppy, your brother must have been the flower
of a dark seed. Your memories are a tapeworm that will

die with you. Don't try to understand or to forgive what should never be forgiven. You are God's child. Believe the promise in rain: there is something new on the way.

New Year's Day, 2017

Five grandchildren who watched crystal glitter
as Times Square's ball dropped are asleep.
To turn the old year's end into a celebration

of my love for them, I said five symbolizes God's
goodness and earth's favor to me. Multiplied
by themselves, they become twenty-five, are

grace upon grace. Two hours into the new year,
checking to be sure that they are breathing,
at the foot of their beds, I reach down to pet

my dog, Bear. His head warm between paws,
no in and out of chest. Nothing. The most stillness
I have ever touched. From across the hall, I had

heard Bear move from one side of their room to
the other, reminding me of my father, his terminal
restlessness in Hospice. There was no moan as Bear

finally unhinged on the floor. A greater pain erases
a lesser one; fear of having children wake to death
of our dog shrouds my heart. They are already being

given a world that is broken. After Charleston, SC,
there is no place to escape evil, hatred, but I want
to create sanctuary. So, December 15, 2016, I turned

off Dylann Roof's trial in Charleston for murdering
nine people who welcomed him to the prayer circle
at Emanuel African Methodist Episcopal Church.

All I can do now is call my sons to smuggle Bear out
for cremation. Four in the morning, the vet hospital,
I can release my tears. I don't save my dog's ashes;

no canister can contain my grief. Trying to get a grip
on the new year's handle, when they get up, how will
I explain to five children why there is no food bowl

to fill, no water dish, no nose beneath their elbow?
I decide it's best to lie, say the hollowing of our hearts
created by Bear's death leaves more room for love,

how anything emptied waits for what comes next.
First it was Bear's hips and then it must have been
the heart—did he forgive the crate? There never

was hunger. If I tell his story over, over, it will
become a snow globe of pain. I have put so many
dogs to sleep, each one's death was a struggle.

Never before have I felt a tug from leash on a collar
that is attached to nothing. There is no body as I open
then close the patio door. Like odor of mint mulled

for juleps, Bear's scent lingers on the couch. His loss
is giant like the claw of a stone crab that is broken off.
Body thrown back into the water, it grows another

which is snapped off. Crippled again, thrown back,
pincers emerge once more. Does the time come when
it will only nurse the wound, cannot grow a new claw?

PAGURUS BERNHARDUS, THE HERMIT CRAB

Low tide, my grandsons turn over rocks
to net crabs for their buckets. I remind them
that hermit crabs breathe through gills, live
only if they are kept damp. To create a pool,
the youngest asks for a shovel and digs a hole
in sand right beside the seawall, out of my sight.
I can't resist a lecture on marine biology.
Hermit crabs have a long, spirally curve

of an abdomen which is soft. To protect it
from gulls, they completely retract into shelter.
Sea snails are a favorite home. Hoping
to lure the boys away from disrupting nature,
I go out to a tide pool in a hollow of granite,
with minnows teeming in feathery seaweed,
feelers of barnacles emerging to filter water
for tiny copepods—empty periwinkle shells

sprout legs and the head of hermit crab emerges,
scuttles through moss. What I thought was
a pebble darts a few inches, stops and it's really
a drab blenny. No way to figure out why some
are aggressive, some peaceful. I'm no Discovery
channel; my grandsons don't follow me. Hearing
their laughter, then *More, More!* I run back to
my chair, look over railing to find them burying

the crabs under dry sand. Startled, I shout *Stop!*
The crabs will die. My oldest grandson grins,
and argues they have a chance to dig out
if they want to save themselves. They look
at their feet and nod as I lecture: In Belgium

and France, farmers still unearth bones curled
into commas in WWII battlefields now gone
to grass, so many bullets, helmets, belt-buckles

that the smell of rust hangs permanently
on the morning dew. To make my grandsons
understand burying crabs is not like a battle
but a massacre, I unfold a picture of boys
their age, July, 2017, *NYT* front page headlines
about Kananga, Democratic Republic
of the Congo. Mass graves are everywhere:
next to a house where a woman is hanging

clothes to dry, in a field where children
kick a rock that rolls like a ball or a head.
Earth that covers bodies has smoothed. Men
in red berets, aviator sunglasses, AK-47s
keep relatives, reporters from unearthing death.
No soldier, no AK-47, the minute I leave the rail,
settle in my seat, my grandsons begin to bury
more crabs—this time they are careful to be silent.

WHAT THE WORLD NEEDS NOW IS *BETA VULGARIS*

At Whole Foods, I don't expect Latin labels,
but I'm horrified to find chard's green rumpled
leaves misplaced in kale. Surely, Amazon would
fire the produce girl so I don't notify a manager.

I can tell a lot about a person based on whether
they know what chard is. Depending on your age,
you might know it as silverbeet, seakale beet,
or perpetual spinach. Ask me, *What is chard?*

I'll know you are not into sustainability, never
shop at farmers' markets. If you're from Vermont,
I pity you—no locavore. Unlike kale, there's no
need to drink it. Chard will make you optimistic,

even ward off seasonal depression. In fact, I am
actually thinking about starting a National Chard
Day in 2019 to improve our country's mental, maybe
even political health. Originally grown as seashore

plants in the Mediterranean, chard has a long history.
Aristotle mentions red-stalked beet chard in 350 B.C.
the botanist Gaspard Bauhin gave it the label Swiss
in *Phytopinax* published in Basel in 1596. Biennial,

edible dark green leaves and red, white or yellow
stalks regenerate even with heavy harvesting.
Chard is a community unto itself. One spear
pushing away from earth gives way to another.

They circle, wagons around the campfire. Older
shoots shelter the young, those about to be born—

so strip only briny-bitter outer ones off crunchy
sweet stems. Let the plant grow from the heart

to ensure survival like that of three ginkgo trees
in Hiroshima. August 6, 1945. The atom bomb.
80,000 died in an instant. Charred, peppered
with glass, clothes melted, tens of thousands

succumbed in the days and months to come.
Three ginkgoes, *hibakujumoku*, the survivor tree,
spread their supple limbs in Shukkeien gardens
of the Hosen-ji and Myojoin-ji temples. These

survivor trees avoided extinction because roots
were underground and spared annihilation.
Within days of the nuclear blast, they'd sprouted
new green shoots. A master of survival, ginkgoes

are in fossils 270 million years old. Now, peace
has come to Hiroshima not by anesthesia of erasure,
but recognition that what has been done cannot
disappear as if it had never been. Interwoven with

the hope that *hibakujumoku* roots bring, delicate
lobes shaped into tiny fans are a promise from
past generations to the world like that of chard
renewing life from its core. Leaves can unfold

like pages of a future where new dreams of peace
aren't blown away but reseeded. With healing will
come a gathering, perhaps releasing a butterfly
taking refuge in the green, allowing it to take wing.

 **II**

How to Survive the 21ˢᵗ Century: Find Poems

When Is Silence a Lie

What does a question mark do?
It looks and acts sort of like an ear,
waiting at the end of a sentence
for an answer. So what is the effect
of a question without a question mark?

Consider, for instance, the jarringly
flat statement, "Where are you going."
The voice, ominously, fails to rise.
Curiosity has been replaced by something
else: terror, accusation, exhaustion.
It's the kind of thing you might hear
at 2 a.m. in a dark room as you try
to sneak out the front door. No answer
is expected. No answer will satisfy.

Do extreme circumstances mitigate lies.
Why was Louis Till, the father of Emmett Till,
court-martialed and hanged in Italy
by the United States Army in 1945? Did he
really commit the crimes he was accused of?
What else might have happened? How deep
do the layers of American injustice run?

Why would anyone reading the tale
today challenge its impartiality.
Will a moment finally emerge in which
a collection of lies offers access to truth.
Some questions have no answers.
Why pretend otherwise?

"New Sentences." By Sam Anderson.
The NYT Magazine. 4/30/2017. P. 15.

THE HOWS AND WHYS OF INVISIBILITY

It is possible to become invisible,
but you must be patient, methodical,
and willing to eat almost anything.
One characteristic spell, recorded
by the British polymath John Aubrey
around 1680, instructs you to begin
by acquiring the severed head
of a man who has committed suicide.

You then bury the head, together with
seven black beans, on a Wednesday
morning before sunrise, and water
the ground for seven days with fine
brandy. On the eighth day, the beans
will sprout, whereupon you must
persuade a little girl to pick and shell
them. Pop one into your mouth,
and you will turn invisible.

If you don't have eight days to wait,
you can, instead, gather water
from a fountain exactly at midnight
(invisibility spells are fetishistic about
time management), bring it to a boil,
and drop in a live black cat. Let it
simmer for twenty-four hours,
fish out whatever remains, throw
the meat over your left shoulder,
then take the bones, and while looking
in the mirror, place them one by one
between the teeth on the left side

of your mouth. You'll know you've
turned invisible when you turn invisible.

"Sight Unseen." By Kathryn Schulz.
The New Yorker. 4/13/2013. P. 75.

DOES THE BALLOON CREW
HAVE A BALLOON CREW?

We contain whole ecosystems
of resistance to ourselves.
I, for instance, have something
strange that happens when
I stand in a high place. It's like
a hot-air-balloon crew in my feet.
When I look over the railing
of the Golden Gate Bridge,
the crew pulls its little flame cord,
and I can feel the basket starting
to rise, a terrifying lifting
sensation at the bottom
of my shoes, and I have to step
quickly away from the edge
and walk off to someplace low.
Such alienation could go on forever.

"New Sentences." By Sam Anderson.
The NYT Magazine. 10/22/2017. P. 15.

FLOATING

If you can flail, you can doggy paddle.
But learning to *float* required a stillness
I didn't have. Even in the shallow end,
with hands supporting my sacrum
I struggled to let my body go limp.

Suddenly, the instruction went from
"go!" to "relax." Face up and staring
at the faraway ceiling, I tried to keep
still, but I was too busy worrying about
my inner ear, which I feared was slowly
filling with pool water. Unable to do
nothing, I tried everything. I inflated
my belly like a balloon, sucking in air
for ballast. I arched my back skyward,
willing myself to levitate. But for every
action, as the law goes, there was an equal
and opposite reaction—in this case sinking.

I was trapped in a cycle of anxiety and
thrashing that had me whipping up water
like a marine Tasmanian Devil rather
than trying to quiet my brain to use floating
to achieve inner peace of doing nothing.

"Floating." By Orr Shtuhl.
The NYT. 1/7/2018. P. 26-7.

How to Be Naked in Public

Begin by practicing in private. Sure,
you can be nude in your own shower,
but how about sitting in the living room
watching TV? How about having dinner?

The first time you strip down in front
of strangers, do so at a specified nudist
destination—a sauna or a beach where
everyone else will also be unclothed.
To be truly at ease, you have to be naked
for yourself, not for the pleasure of others.

The moments before disrobing are always
the most anxious. On average, it takes
an hour for people to get comfortable
and begin frolicking like 5-year-olds
running around the backyard. Choose
your activities carefully. Swimming is
the easiest for beginners. Volleyball and
other jumping sports are more challenging.
Yoga can be particularly intimidating.

Don't be surprised if you occasionally
experience phantom clothes. Initially,
the parts of your body you are the most
insecure about— genitals, breasts, hips,
moles, whatever—will loom large.
You'll imagine people are looking at
that thing, but they're not. Still, expect
some wandering eyes, including your own.
Looking is normal, but don't stare.

"How to Be Naked in Public." By Malia
Wollan. *The NYT Magazine.* 8/23/2015. P. 19.

SEVENTY-FIVE IS A BAD AGE

I tend to get depressed at twilight.
The transition makes me sad—
the end of the light, the beginning
of the dark. It's somehow worse
than total blackness, to have
that last bit of the day, to watch it
shift and dim. Once it's gone,
it's gone—that's the world you
live in now. But before that comes
the watching it go. There is something
absurd, of course, about assigning
value to an age so confidently,
as if it were an objective fact,
as if it didn't depend almost entirely
on context. In that notorious part
of woods where clear paths disappear,
you are suffering changes: work, body,
moods shift from one thing to something
else. Elders become truly elderly.
Everywhere you turn, there are twilights.

"Thirty-five Is a Bad Age." By Sam Anderson.
The NYT Magazine. 7/1/2018. P. 13.

An Older Woman's Guide
to Aphrodisiacs: Oysters

Above all, never shuck when you're angry
or frustrated. If you're flustered, breathe
in and out, roll your shoulders, then begin.
You're going to butcher it the first time:
it's O.K. A shucker should be careful
not to puncture the organism inside.
Don't spill any juices or leave behind bits
of shrapnel. An opened oyster should look
unmolested, like it doesn't know it's missing
its shell. First get acquainted with basic
anatomy. Oysters have two distinct halves.
Gently slip in. Wiggle as you would a stubborn
key until it opens a little. Slide your knife
along lids tenderly, running your blade
under the oyster until it's free-floating in its
own juices. Brush off any tidbits before eating.

"How to Shuck an Oyster." By Malia Wollan.
The NYT Magazine. 7/1/2018. P. 21.

How to Collect Seashells

Search at night to avoid competition.
Storms wash more shells ashore in winter;
pick a spot and settle in. Rather than hoard,
take only beautiful specimens. Make sure
the shell is uninhabited with spiral-shaped
gastropods. You should be able to see
the creature, vulnerable to pollution and
ocean acidification. Your urge to collect
calcium-carbonate dwellings can serve as
a gateway drug. Once you love shells,
learn to care about animals that make them.

"How to Collect Seashells." By Malia Wollan.
The NYT Magazine. 5/27/2018. P. 19.

How to Preserve a Species: Teach a Bird to Talk

A single parrot cannot forage for fruit
and watch for predators at the same time;
it depends on its chittering flock
for protection. Therefore, to teach a bird
that can talk—parrots, parakeets or mynas,
for example—to talk, find one that
for lack of better options thinks of you
as its flock. Don't get an old disappointed
bird. Buy a baby bird. Specifically opt
for one bred in captivity (or rescued)
rather than one snatched from the wild,
spending as much time as possible
the first several months talking
to your bird in gentle tones, reassuring
it as you would a young child. Don't
hurry them to talk. They need to feel
security in the heart first. Once the bird
has confidence in you as a companion
and reliable food source, start repeating
simple phrases. First you say,

You are very good.
How are you my dear?
I love you.

Many trainers reward learning with nuts
or seeds; though they occasionally
treat the bids to a sip of milky chai tea.
As a bird starts showing aptitude,
ratchet up the difficulty and repetition
by recording your voice and playing

it back to the bird for up to three hours
a day. A person will be bored by this.
But a bird will never bore.

"How to Teach a Bird to Talk." By Malia
Wollan. *The NYT Magazine.* 3/15/2015. P. 30.

Nuclear Mindfulness

Some mindfulness exercises
for the thirty minutes between
the launch of a nuclear ballistic missile
and its detonation in your city:

No matter how you choose to spend
the last thirty minutes of your life,
one thing's for certain—you're going
to be breathing. You can count
your breaths if that helps you to relax,
but it may increase tension if you find
yourself counting down. It might
be tempting to check social media
to see how world leaders are interpreting
the coming apocalypse. Practice
putting down the phone; you may be
surprised at how logging off allows you
to "log in" to the rapidly crumbling world
around you. Choose an object in view
and take a moment to observe it closely.
This could be the pattern on your rug,
a roommate loading a gun, or even
the increasingly bright night sky. Once
the power grid goes out, you're only
a few minutes away from annihilation.

Light a scented candle, sit in a chair,
and watch the candle. Notice the flame
in its simplicity and ponder the ironic fact
that humanity has reached its demise
using the same intelligence with which

it mastered fire. Make sure to find
a chair that helps you practice good posture.

"Nuclear Mindfulness." By Ethan Kuperberg.
The New Yorker. 10/9/2017. P. 31.

FIRE AND ICE

Some say the world will end in fire,
Some say in ice
    —Robert Frost

Baked Alaska is a simple ice-cream cake,
but with the tension of a good novel
(will the delicate protagonist—the ice cream—
survive the flames?) and the beauty of a poem.

A work of art. Nothing could be further
from the truth. It's all craft. And a lot of it!
If you find meaning in painstaking details,
you will find the project rewarding,
especially because you can set it on fire and
clap and giggle and then eat the damned thing.

So maybe it's not at all like a poem where
you do all that exacting work but then
at the end realize it ought to be torched,
and you go to bed without applause
and still hungry to boot. Even in craft,
there's room for flourish; the opportunity
to let loose here lies in the meringue.

Piping the meringue with a closed-star tip
makes myriad gorgeous ridges that toast dark
and dramatic, leaving negative white space
in the divots. Unlike an actual work of art—
a painting, say—you can erase what
doesn't work. Just re-pipe the meringue.

You can even fail completely and still win,
because no one will ever send you a letter

of rejection over your sorry meringue,
as they would your sagging prose.

"Fire and Ice." By Gabrielle Hamilton.
The NYT. 12/1/2017. P. 28.

How to Avoid Icebergs

The thing you need most in iceberg infested
waters is fear. Without trepidation, you'll end
up like the Titanic. As glaciers melt, more icebergs
calve into the sea. Greenland is now losing
an average of 303 billion tons of ice
a year. Always have at least one person with
binoculars on the lookout. These hulking
chunks of ice are usually easy
to spot. Give them a wide berth: 90 percent
of their mass is underwater. They can roll
and break apart and make a huge shipping
vessel feel like a dory. Keep a distance
of between 1.5 and 3 miles. Be extra
cautious around so-called bergy bits:
those car-to house-size hunks that fall off
and bob in water down wind. If you manage
to successfully dodge an iceberg, don't talk
about the fact that you have been lucky.
When you do that, you become vulnerable.

"How to Avoid Icebergs." By Malia Wollan.
The NYT Magazine. 4/21/2017. P. 30.

How to Survive Falling Through Ice Trying to Cross a Border in Winter

You have more time than you think.
You'll gasp for breath and begin
to hyperventilate. Don't thrash.
Remember the 1-10-1 principle:
One minute to get control
of your breathing. Ten minutes
of meaningful movement. One hour
before you become unconscious.
Nobody is dead until warm and dead.

Below 86 degrees, you will probably
be unconscious, but not necessarily
lifeless. People have been revived
from as low as 56.7 degrees. You
might live for hours if you can avoid
drowning, but that takes some planning.

Look around: Where is the thickest ice?
You'll want to face the way you came.
Kick using your arms to pull yourself out.
If you feel too weak to continue,
lay your arms across ice and remain still.
You want your jacket to freeze in place
so that when you lose consciousness,
you'll be held there, your head above
the water. Frozen prone at the lip
of the hole, you'll remain visible and
can be saved long after you black out.

"How to Survive Falling Through the Ice."
By Malia Wollan. *The NYT Magazine.*
2/14/2016. P. 23.

KEEPING COOL

Tell nobody what you are doing.
Even your loved ones—especially
your loved ones—must be kept
in the dark. If it comes to a choice
between smoking and talking,
smoke. Dress well but without
ostentation. Wear a raincoat,
buttoned and belted, regardless
of whether there is rain. Any revolver
should be kept, until you need it,
in the pocket of the coat. Finally,
before you leave, put your hat on.
If you don't have a hat, you can't go.

"Keeping Cool." By Anthony Lane.
The New Yorker. 5/1/2017. P. 70.

How to Cross the Rio Grande River, Mexico to Texas, if There Is No Guard Standing out in the Blazing Sun

Even shallow water can knock you off your feet.
First spend some time watching it. Explore
the edge. Throw a stick in. If the floating
stick moves faster than you can walk, find
a wider, shallower crossing where the current
is slower. Always look downstream for hazards.
You don't want to go over a rapid or a waterfall.
If you're stymied, wait to see if the water drops.
Once you've found the right spot, keep your shoes
on. Unbuckle your backpack: if you fall in,
you'll need to wriggle free. Find a sturdy branch
and use it and your two feet to make a tripod.
Always keep two points of contact on the ground.
If the water rises about your knees, back out.
Despite your inevitable desire to press on,
you may need to wait a day, or even turn around.

"How to Ford a River." By Malia Wollan.
The NYT Magazine. 3/27/2016. P. 23.

HOW TO TAKE A PUNCH

Don't close your eyes. Try to avoid
even blinking. Watch the fist come
and learn from it. Keep in constant
motion but maintain a centered stance.
A blow to the face looks bad, creates
the perception that you're losing,
particularly if you bleed or your head
flies backward. Whatever you do,
don't get angry. Stay in the present
moment to endure. Don't get distracted.
Sometimes an adversary will wink,
blow a kiss, grin wildly or stick out
her tongue. If you're hitting or being hit
in a psychologically messy state, stop.

"How to Take a Punch." By Malia Wollan.
The NYT Magazine. 5/15/2016. P. 33.

How to Get Rid of Lice

There's no reason to be ashamed.
The sesame-seed-size insects don't
care if you're rich or poor, clean or dirty,
rural or urban. Girls are more prone
to lice than boys and African-Americans
are far less likely to host the bugs. Make
sure you're dealing with head lice and not,
say, dandruff. Look for oval-shaped eggs,
called nits, firmly attached to the hair shaft
close to the scalp. You'll need an insecticide.
Don't apply mayonnaise, vodka, WD-40,
kerosene. You're not the first to confront
the itch, and you won't be the last. Parents,
especially wealthier ones, become irate
over live outbreaks, yelling at school nurses
and even janitors. Don't do that.

"How to Get Rid of Lice." By Malia Wollan.
The NYT Magazine. 5/14/2017. P. 19.

Dear Type-A Parent

Congratulations! The application on behalf
of your child for the pre-kindergarten class
at The School has been rejected. This permits
you to begin the Type-A Parent Appeal Process,
the kind of challenge that makes the Type-A
parent's life worth living. Necessary forms:
A hand-delivered letter on the stationery
of a New Jersey waste-haulage firm, folded
around a rock and thrown through the stained
glass window of The School's library will secure
you the pamphlet, "Explaining the Appeal Process."
If, like many type-A parents, you find this option
unsatisfactory, you may take the following steps:

1. Threaten to introduce bedbugs to blankie-storage
cubbies if you are not granted an immediate
personal interview with the full Board of Trustees.

2. Send money. The School cannot bow to parental
pressure, of course, but will accept cash in exchange
for reconsideration of your child's application.

As a prospective parent, which of the following
do you think are the most important to maintaining
The School's well-being and competitive edge?
(Check all that apply.)

Funding a new gymnasium   _____
Spring class trip to Borneo   _____
New faculty sauna   _____

Gift-giving children are preferred to gifted children.

"Dear Type-A Parent." By Bruce McCall.
The New Yorker. 2/8/2010. P. 31.

I'm Good

Nobody *smokes* marijuana anymore.
Everyone's vaping it. Or eating, drinking,
sipping, dabbing, sucking on lozenges,
chewing on gum, applying unguents
or a drop of a cannabis-infused tincture
under the tongue where it is absorbed
within minutes producing an invisible,
odorless, private high. The drug
of lazy stoners is the "wellness" drug
of tomorrow. It's a cure-all for an anxious,
tech-addled society—a salve for every
ailment, a balm for every mood,
ibuprofen meets a glass of red wine cut
with Prozac and a hint of Deepak Chopra,
all delivered to your door.
It's just a merchandiser's dream.

"I'm Good: Pot Start-Ups Pass Up the Joint."
By Farhad Manjoo. *The NYT.* 1/25/2018. P. B1.

THE PAST SLEDS BEHIND

What an excellent verb: sleds.
What a weirdly specific way
to visualize time, the entire history
of everything from formless abstraction
(an energy field, a tidal wave, a void)
into a kid on a toboggan, pompom
bouncing yarnily on top of a winter hat.
The past becomes perky and alive
and attentive, always on your heels
as you trek perpetually forward.
A lifelong mope, I imagine the past
very differently—a kind of ocean,
always running backward toward
low tide, receding, draining away
from me, and I stand stuck on the edge
of its shore, knowing that it contains
everything I have ever known—my father
and mother, black dog and orange cat—
but all of that is suspended in water
that rushes away from me, and I will
never enter it, will never recover what
has sunk. There will be no high tide.
But, language is powerful. The past
can be a sled. Just turn around and look.

"New Sentences." By Sam Anderson.
The NYT Magazine. 6/3/2018. P 13.

III

COLLEGE OF CHARLESTON, SC,
AUGUST 21, 2017, THE SOLAR ECLIPSE

Is the theft of the day like theft of identity?
Luminous umbilical cord eight minutes
and 19 seconds long—the time it takes light
to travel to earth from the sun. Total solar eclipse,

moon covering the sun, a lifeline is severed,
tide of darkness swallows the planet. First totality:
Salem, WA 10:15 a.m, Pacific time. The moon
standing up to the sun over a seventy-mile wide

beveled ribbon was a curtain racing toward me—
1,462 mph in Kentucky where I'm from, picking
up to 1,502 mph arriving 2:50 p.m. Eastern time.
No shadow bands on ground, nothing. Clouded out.

Weather, a roulette-wheel, I had pictured Regulus,
brightest star in Leo stepping from a robe of twilight
over the sun's shoulder—then Mercury, Mars
and Venus inching out of deepening gloom. No

first contact with the moon grazing then eating away
the sun. No Baily's beads of randomly spaced light
in an arc connecting crescent tips, sunlight shining
through valleys of the moon. Second contact. Gloom.

No night slamming me. No black hole blacker than
black fringed like a flapper in white fire. The moment
of totality was the time to scream in ecstasy but not
at clouds to dissolve. No wordless solidarity. What

else could I do but pop open a Corona, the eclipse
beer of choice? C of C students around me, I didn't
want to date myself, had ear buds in listening
to *Dark Star* by Grateful Dead and *Earth's Creation*

by Stevie Wonder. Only the best eclipse glasses
for me—Celestron Eclipsmart Power Viewers,
certification ISO 12312-2. I am a child of light.
When the sun came back from totality, I had planned

to cry—and I did, in anger. Veiled, the crescent
appeared, not burning bright as the first line of *Genesis:*
In the beginning, God created the heavens and the earth.
Heading past Fort Sumter across slivers of wetlands,

the Atlantic, the eclipse ended at sunset near Africa.
No awe, no totality. Language was not ripped away,
no lifeline severed. Ripping off paper glasses, I am
not surprised to find myself standing by a tombstone:

> *Near this spot is buried,*
> *Elizabeth Jackson,*
> *Mother of President Andrew Jackson.*
> *She gave her life cheerfully for*
> *the independence of her country,*
> *on an unrecorded date in Nov, 1781,*
> *and to her son Andy this advice:*
> *'Andy, never tell a lie*
> *nor take what is not your own,*
> *nor sue for slander,*
> *settle those cases yourself.'*

No birth or death date, Elizabeth, where are words
recording your life? Thirst for your history quenched

by your son's fame, not even a church dress, when you
died, your friend Agnes Barton slipped hers on you,

buried you on a hill in an unmarked grave about
a mile from forks of Meeting and Kingstree Roads.
Was there nothing to say? Born in Ireland sometime
in 1740, married, you may have sucked icicles

to ease nausea on the ship sailing to America in 1765,
a Presbyterian escaping persecution. Just twenty-nine,
Andrew's father died three weeks before he was born.
Never again in your own home, raising your two sons

as housekeeper for your invalid sister, Jane, you had
nightly buckets of urine, scrub rags, stained sheets,
iron pots of mutton broth. No granite carving that rain
could smooth. No medals, praise for your courage,

traveling forty miles to Camden, SC with British
prisoners to swap for your sons Robert and Andrew
who had smallpox. No way for your son to find
your bones, even place a rose on a forgotten hillock

for you, a patriot who died from ship's fever you caught
nursing American soldiers held on prison ships moored
in Charleston's harbor. I have no wreath to give you now.
Your stone is the eclipse I had not come to see.

PERSEUS AND THE GORGON (C.1898)

Musée Camille Claudel, Nogent-sur-Seine, France

I.

Catalogue rolled in hand from the museum built in 2017
around your childhood home, I sit to rest my knee

before starting through forty-three of your sculptures,
beginning with *Old Helene*, your family housekeeper

with wrinkles deeper than mine. Next, *Young Roman*,
your brother Paul at sixteen posed as a young Caesar.

I linger by *Abandonment:* two lovers cling suspended
in an embrace. Your hands went beneath skin to shape

desire of the man who kneels, straining to reach a woman
who bends down for his kiss. Placed so close together,

a bronze bust of your lover, Auguste Rodin, is jarring.
Is his head severe, menacing because he would not get

down on one knee, wedding ring in hand? At the end
of the museum tower, I confront Perseus looming over

six feet tall, brandishing Medusa's head you sculpted
with your own features. He is gazing at what once was

the bronze shield that he used to mirror Medusa's
paralyzing stare and petrify the Gorgon with its own

reflection. Camille, were Medusa's snakes already
writhing like tortured thoughts inside your head?

II.

1883. Rodin became your teacher: not quite twenty,
you his muse, his mistress. You must have made
the forty-three-year-old hands that molded *The Kiss*
and *The Thinker* shake, the clothes melt from his body.
Even with a beret like a mushroom cap on his head,

Auguste caused a fever to trip the rhythm jump roping
your heart. Calling you *Mademoiselle Say* for C,
in later years, you would label him *The Ferret* from
Latin *furittus* meaning *little thief*. You knew to drink
with your mouth around a wine bottle to arouse him.

Rodin's body said *Trespass* even though he would not
leave Rose Beuret, mother of his son. How fine it would
have been, even briefly, to be the center of his attention.
Losing Rodin to Rose again, again, his absence greater
every time, anger kneaded you, your ability to estrange

in direct proportion to depth of the need for his love.
Intense and sensual, you never could be the obedient
student Rodin wanted, your style not as complex,
turbulent as his with its deeply pocketed surface he
gouged into clay. Something electric under your skin,

was he your Perseus, freezing you into a living statue,
the perfect model but never quite a woman with interior
need he would not fill? No way to prepare for the erasure,
you could not tourniquet your nerves after a miscarriage.
Auguste was afraid of creating another child; sex ended.

I stop to rest again, transfixed by your *Old Age* where
you mirrored the final rupture with him: a young woman,

naked, stretches out on her knees, arms lifted imploring
the nude man in the center who has dropped her hand
and turned his back to be led away wrapped in cloaked

arms of an old woman, Rose Beuret, with features like
a vulture. A visual symbol of your rage, you must have
imagined them, birds of prey mating with their talons
clenched face to face, plummeting down in a spiral,
knowing how to part over and over before they hit rock.

III.

Already detesting you because as an artist, you behaved
like a man, even more agitated by your affair with Rodin,
your mother razored your face from photographs. For her,
everything was black or white, flat or upright. You were
asked to leave home. Depressed, you now had to live alone.
In your Paris studio, winters buttoned you in a dark coat
billowing over your ankles. Like Pandora who left *Elpis*,
hope, at the bottom of a *pithos*, a jar big enough for burial,
dreams of praise for your sculptures unearthed by spring
pulled you under even when Claude Debussy pursued you,
kept a replica of *The Waltz* in his studio until his death.
Your romantic life over at 30; Debussy wrote *I weep for
the disappearance of the Dream of this Dream.* Creating
a model of Perseus in 1898, were you announcing not just
the end with Rodin but of your career as artist by replacing
Medusa's face with your own self portrait? Unlike Perseus
who held your face crowned with snakes up in his hand
like a trophy, Rodin could not sever the genius in your head
thrumming behind your eyes pulsing into your fingers.

IV.

Your mother disowned you, said you'd made your bed
with Auguste, now you could lie in it alone. Abandoned,
no wonder you were paranoid, accused Rodin of stealing

sketches, of conspiring to kill you. In despair of having
your talent celebrated, you destroyed much of your work,
even the plaster cast of Perseus in 1912. Your father

who loved you and supported your life as artist, died
in 1913. Your mother and brother didn't tell you, didn't
invite you to the funeral, waited only eight days after

his death to commit you to a mental asylum. Year after
year, doctors tried to convince them you were sane
and should be free, should be taken home, but year after

year your mother and brother refused. No sentence you
could hold up as proof of sanity could splinter their hearts.
Confined for 30 years until your death at 78, your mother

never visited you and your brother Paul, who had said
I am the only genius in this family, came 7 times, always
referred to you in past tense. Did your teeth stay clenched

for days after his visits or did your mind knit at new words
after your mother's death trying to persuade your brother
to release you? Like a mare on a carousel that never moves,

head arched ready for the jump that never comes, everyday,
more turns, you couldn't unbolt your nerves from the up
and down. There is no way for me to imagine the mornings,

afternoons, nights of living 30 sane years in an insane asylum.
No doctor recorded what you might have said; your mother
didn't allow you to receive or send mail. I hope your brother

did not tell you Rodin married Rose Beuret before they both
died in 1917. On your breasts, the claustrophobia of his hands
tattooed into your flesh, was thought of Rodin like a male

cricket at night, running the top of one wing along teeth
at the bottom of the other, sound relentless and unending,
as if the insect was scraping marrow from your bones?

V.

It must have been the worst for your hands that had no plaster,
clay, onyx or marble. Nothing to braid from the fabric of living.
To keep your fingers busy, did you knit afghans to wear down
the clock, peel apples in the kitchen? As a girl rowing a boat,
you learned the most important thing is not to think, the art
of holding together in abeyance. Your heart a metronome
keeping time, like Antonio Stradivari who played his violin
to the pine trees, did your hands shape air into torso, thigh,
neck? Surely your body sloughed the idea of home. What

you could not have missed was a mother who never gave
you a bath, a prayer each night to keep you safe. At her death,
in 1929, your friend, sculptor Jessie Lipscomb could finally
visit you and insisted that "it was not true" you were insane.
Your future contracted and would never expand. No periodic
cicada living underground as a nymph, you would not emerge
in 13 to 17 years, but died October 19, 1943. At the end,
like a dried hide nailed to the wall, no way to know if a hand
closed your eyes at the asylum in Montfavet—your brother

was not present at your death or funeral and never claimed
your body. Finally, your remains were buried at the asylum
mixed into a communal grave with bones of the destitute.
Returned to clay you shaped as a child, you are exiled forever
from the earth where you played in Villeneuve-sur-Fere.
In Musée Camille Claudel with statues I can't touch, there's
no place to mourn your flesh. Nothing is left of your body like
pieces of Percy Shelley's skull in the NYC Public Library or
a walking stick Virginia Woolf carried to water's edge. Nothing.

Number Fifty-two: Winifred Benham, Hartford, Connecticut, October 7, 1697

Joseph, my husband, could not hold his tongue,
said selectmen were no more fit for office than dogs,
threatened to shoot a neighbor who'd named me *witch*.
Ours was prime land on the east side of Main Street
just south of Center Street in Wallingford. Watching

the surveyor and tax assessor finger pears, spit grape
seeds around my orchard, I knew to train for holy water.
Lowered in a barrel, my life, our six acres would be taken
if I was damned, gnawed by demons that caused me to rise.
Pulled down to blackness, encircled by the hand of God,

three minutes would prove my innocence. My accusers
rehearsed their lines: John Moss, 15, only grandson
of Wallingford's commissioner and Elizabeth Lathrop,
19, daughter of the New London Court judge, testified
I had frequently and sorely afflicted parts of their bodies

too private for inspection. Charges were posted: I read
Shakespeare, not scripture; I appeared as apparitions,
allowing Satan to take my form. Stripped in court,
searched for signs of possession, stretch marks where
the devil must have suckled were found. They matched

a row of spots that appeared while bathing the corpse
of the infant son of Joseph Royce, a founding father
in Wallingford. Other physical evidence was Winifred,
my daughter. At thirteen, she could only be a child
of the devil, being born so late when I was forty-five.

Attending more than thirty trials, I had seen women
who could not sink, struggling upward to surface
for air the rope would suck away. I witnessed women
forgotten a minute too long. Innocent, but hanging
in holy water, no breath of an angel for breeze, dresses

undulated as if to Purcell. I prepared for the judge,
whose brother lived across the street from us, to become
distracted, perhaps by a fit of coughing or a baby teething.
Declared unclean like the cormorant in *Deuteronomy*,
I learned from gutting the bird how the rounded sea

pebbles in its stomach served as a diver's weight.
Forgetting my skill as seamstress, the judge didn't slit
oval panels on my skirt for rocks or pull the braiding.
I had prepared my answer: bombast, your honor, cotton
stuffing inserted to bulge my dress in Elizabethan fashion.

In bed, I practiced kicking with feet tied, learned how
to count out three minutes, studied where women's
fingers rested when bound to their sides. Burning, lungs
were about to consume me. Pulling the two cords
I had left next to my hands to release slip stitches

binding smooth stones, I kicked to surface, to salvation.
Under holy water, thinking of the judge above me, I found
a darkness I would grow into. Unable to nail my world
back into shape like I did the arbor in my garden the judge
could not confiscate in God's name, I craved a reason,

an explanation to justify my trial. Reading Milton's
description of Satan in *Paradise Lost* who *sat like
a cormorant* in the Tree of Life preparing to work
mischief in the Garden of Eden, I slicked my hair back
like a tulip, used India ink to cover the gray. Deliberate

as Joseph unbuttoning my blouse each night, I wanted
my neighbors to watch me reach up to pluck down stars
as if they were eyes, then bend to uproot ferns with shovels,
sometimes with spoons. Crushing bottles in my hand
to seed the garden, I thought of their swelling nerves, joints

aching as they swiveled while my hatred worked its way
into their hearts. Rubbing my belly while mixing tea, I
added herbs for stomach venom, roots for fever to shake
awake mouths blubbering in sleep. Time surely will
swallow up my place in history as the last witch tried

in Connecticut, but the sight of a cormorant, shining
like a black angel struggling to fly, will keep alive
the cry of a believer fallen. With no final word, unable
to make up one truth to give my daughter a sliver
of comfort, each October, I tell her to imagine God

at an easel, painting leaves sunflower, crimson, ochre,
copper, sienna. Freezing them to edge in crystal, a master
with a trained eye, the artist stands back deciding what
to crop from the canvas, which stand of forest should be
cut and which trees will move to the center of the frame.

MAY 17, 1720: SUPERIOR COURT JUSTICE COUNSELS ELIZABETH ATWOOD IN HIS CHAMBERS BEFORE SENTENCING HER TO HANG

If any woman be delivered of any issue of her body, male or female, which, if it were born alive, should by law be a bastard and that she endeavors privately, either by drowning or secret burying hereof, or any other way, either by herself or the procuring of others, so to conceal the death thereof that it may not come to light, whether it was born alive or not, but be concealed, in every such case the other so offending shall suffer death as in case of murder, except such mother can make proof by one witness at the least that the child whose death was by her so intended to be concealed was born dead.
—Massachusetts Provincial
Laws, 1692–93, Chapter 19, Section 7.

In the final conversation about Judgment, you will be the first
to get to give your version. Quivering to hear your name,

Elizabeth, remember scarlet in the live oaks was blinding
that first day when the bench you sat on was just a bench.

Hair thin as dune grass, I believed I had roots, that your beauty
would not be small waves coming in with the tide, sucking

my clothes. I left, came back. Left, came back, hiding under
branches so God would not see me, thinking how cool, green

the garden must have been. Michael Wigglesworth, I wrote
in my diary, *for admiring myself, I loathe myself.* Your house,

a whistle only I could hear, the gray cat was the other life I saw.
Pressing my stomach against your spine, your breasts cupped

in my palms were better than any hope of afterlife. I fell asleep
in your bed, awakened to a gull startling me like a rusty hinge.

Fog hung like a bed sheet. I was in the wrong house, could not
find my clothes, my wife. The first time, I told her I had been

praying deep in briar, then it was the bay gleaming like tar,
the smell of the Atlantic that drew me. Those dawns spread like

a rash, but sunset was your menstrual smear until there was snow
filling, white, white, swelling to banks. I never wanted the child

to be the sum of our parts, rounded into an irregular face almost
human. Even under oath, I knew you would not name me father.

This court will never prosecute me for fornication or adultery.
Our bastard's red hair above my earlobes would have spoken

our sin in each street of Ipswich. You refused to kill what love
had created. I had to do what you should have done. Surely,

Elizabeth, you must want to leave me in peace. When we go out
of this room, it will be time for you to say what you have to say.

The courtroom stilled by our entry, even God will be looking
down with interest. Like ships dry docked in Salem's harbor,

or dogs with heads cocked, Essex County's women are hushed
to hear loneliness, hurt, a poem you might have written. Spinster,

twenty-eight, you slept with no husband's arm across your hip.
Ipswich's men understand you were filled with sin, with desire.

I am trying to give you a defense. Plead insanity or great
emotional stress during pregnancy. Crazed by pain, you didn't

know what you were doing. Whisper ignorance, delirium,
or illness at birth. All are legal excuses for fatal neglect. Fitting

the weak nature you share with all women, claim inexperience.
Because of incessant crying, you dropped our son or placed him

in an unheated attic, fell asleep and had no money to pay for
a doctor. You could have overlaid such a small body, smothered

it in bed. Just last year, I acquitted an exhausted mother because
her infant slipped from her unsteady grasp, fell into the privy.

Using gloves, I was careful, didn't leave marks on our son's
neck to condemn you. No recorded testimony, the boy was

already dead when your stepmother came and cleared herself
by giving this court the date of birth. February the 20th is branded

into me. Willful, unrepentant, you wear your blood-stained dress
to court, but will not acknowledge your sin. Elizabeth, how can

I save you? Don't ask me for what purpose and quote St. Paul,
I Corinthians 15: *Flesh and blood cannot inherit the kingdom.*

Ink dripping from my pen, you give me no choice but to date
your death warrant: June 23, 1720. As the chief magistrate

for Massachusetts Superiour Court of Judicature, Assize and
General Goal Delivery, it's my duty to lead you to Mile Lane

and High Road, watch Sheriff Denison hang you at Gallows' Lot
on Pingrey's Plain. Elizabeth, raise your clenched hand to me,

uncurl it slowly, release me at least from your judgment. Think
of my days closed up in this room after you are gone. Imagine

the ache in my lungs, like a right whale wheezing in dark, each
breath in deep water held a very long time. Spring will resurrect

our first mornings. I will peer from attic slats, not knowing
one day to the next, if I will stride around a judge, vivid like God,

shoulders in the clouds or be staring into that little elastic face.
If I take a walk into a pasture, the scent of milk on your breasts

might come to me. Think of the place in my body where the past
with you will thorn, rise sharp as the question of what will

happen to me if I am found out. Sins deducted from graces,
you will go to heaven, but I will be roped to this earth, knotted

by memory, by the fear of last breath: the noose on your throat,
my hands like a baptism chain circling the neck of our son.

PROUD FLESH: MARY WAITS FOR SHELLEY
ON THE GULF OF SPEZIA'S SHORE

I. Day One: July 8, 1822.
Percy Bysshe Shelley and Edward Williams
sail off on their open boat

Sudden, violent, but brief, this summer squall is over.
Until I catch sight of the *Don Juan's* sails, I'll stay.
If I hadn't experienced so much death, I would never
believe you and Edward could both be swept overboard.
Always more certain than I, you dismissed my fears
for your safety. I think of you at nineteen in Devonshire

on the beach at Lynmouth kneeling at sunrise, again
at sunset, launching toy boats you'd waterproofed
with wax and masted with sticks. Each cargoed
your *A Declaration of Rights* into the Bristol Channel.
It was summer, 1812, and a half million soldiers
of Napoleon's *Grande Armee* marched Europe in

a doomed Russian campaign. Sure your message
would change the world if it could but reach it,
you also freed hot-air balloons you had made
from silk to canopy skies of Wales and Ireland.
Gusting into one another, I was sixteen when we met;
my body turned traitor to my mind. Already pregnant,

pinned by centrifugal force, I still remember the date,
July 28, 1814, when you orbited me from England
into six weeks of France, Switzerland and Germany.
Desire bursting us, at the beginning of our flight from those
who condemned us, I tried to live without restraint, not be
warden of your heart. I vowed marriage wouldn't become

a sepulcher for its eternity; I wasn't prepared for your body
next to mine to curl, stretch in a different way causing you
to confess that another woman had melted walls I believed
would hold. At first, our combat was sweet; I grew tired
of escaping creditors by moving from town to town,
of the scent, the hair other women left in sheets for me

to wash. You asked me to be brave, be rational and I was.
Then you asked for more strength; I didn't have it. I began
to believe our bed was dreaming on its own. I would not
sleep there. Feeling between us died. When we walked
to find the thin mountain air you needed to breathe, water
never cascaded to blind me, like you did, but seethed

in rivulets, rock filled streams. For the last two years, settled
in Pisa, you were happier. Unwilling to talk about the loss
of our three children, you thought only of poetry, as Hogg said,
*in season and out of season, at table, in bed, and especially
during a walk.* There were little pleasures— wing shadows,
long grass, how you unfolded your body from a chair, how

you'd slip stray hair behind my ear as my mother might have.
I like to remember the ferry ride circling close by Bellagio,
afternoons on Lake Como. It's been eight years since we met.
I'm twenty-four, you are not quite thirty. If you return, we might
begin again, passion like a current. If not, I have our son Percy.
I won't restring my heart or allow my flesh to betray me again.

II. Day Two: July 9, 1822.
Mary Shelley thinks of her husband's other women

My hand a hat for my eyes, even though I stand here to watch
for you to wash ashore, I will not miss your body—it's belonged
to so many others. I won't speak of virtue knowing those who
have never been tempted by one as beautiful as you, Percy,

are too fond of the word. Again, you have abandoned me,
casting off with Edward in the *Don Juan*, the name a perfect fit
for you. I begged you not to leave me with Edward's common
law wife, Jane. You admired her free spirit, describing marriage

as a *most despotic, most unrequired fetter*, with me as shackle.
To Jane (The keen stars were twinkling), love notes labeled lyrics
did not fool me any more than lines you wrote in Bay of Lerici:
Bright Wanderer, fair coquette of Heaven, / to whom alone it has

been given / to change and be adored forever. You poured out
kisses to any woman who thirsted. First, Harriet, who, like me,
was sixteen when you met and then married her to keep her
innkeeper father from forcing her to go to away school. Only

now do I understand how cruel it was to invite Harriet to come
in the role of sister when you left her to flee with me. I can mark
almost every year of our life together with death. October, 1816:
my half-sister Fanny Imlay took an overdose of laudanum. I

knew it was because of unrequited love for you. That December,
Harriet, shunned because she was an abandoned woman but still
your wife, was pregnant by an unknown lover. With no bridge
to cross, she drowned herself in Hyde Park's Serpentine Lake

in London. There were other women you loved too hastily,
too easily. I never knew the name of Elena's mother, the baby
in Naples, you "adopted" and then left, dead at one and a half.
Did *Stanzas Written in Dejection—December 1818, near Naples*

purge you of these deaths as water now cleanses your flesh?
When you wrote the poem I could find no mention of Elena,
the suicide of Harriet, or our own two dead daughters. But
I circled then counted the pronouns: you used *I* eleven times.

III. Day Three: July 10, 1822.
Remembering the faces of children, Mary keeps vigil

As if fixated on your mouth trying to catch last breath,
I can't look away from waves edging shore. On the underside
of water, have you been pocketed like a stone? Keeping me
company today are mouths of children, still wet and mewling.

Premature, our first daughter lived twelve days. One year later
in 1816, I gave birth to William. September 1818, our Clara
was dead at one, followed in less than nine months by William,
your *Willmouse*, taken by malaria at three. Percy Florence was

born in November, 1819. After my miscarriage in spring, 1820,
I was the only one to console Claire at the death of Allegra,
her daughter by Byron who had sent the girl, barely four,
to an Italian convent in Bagnacavallo. She was dead at five.

After Harriet's suicide, we married at once, but courts denied
you custody of your children —*morally unfit* the judge said.
Ianthe and Charles, placed with foster parents, are alive today.
The motor of it all, it was as if you cared nothing for life

outside our bedroom. Water sweeping this shore of pails and
shovels, you returned for the next day of castles, sure other
children would be born and come with you to build them.
I have read the heart is a pump made of chambers, a muscle

that tightens then releases blood to be oxygenated, returning
it emptied. In ventricles, mine must also hold memory of anger
aroused by your words: *I fall upon the thorns of life! I bleed!*
My blood disgusted you. I was the one to miscarry, give birth

four times, and dress three of our children in burial clothes.
I was no surgeon, could not make an incision in my heart

and extract your words, but even when all those bodies lay
between us, somehow, Percy, you were never irredeemable.

IV. Day Four: July 11, 1882.
Mary Shelley plans her future

You were always one to defy current. I mark erosion,
flotsam of grass on the beach, but not the ballooning
of your body. You will not be bothered by bad weather
or my moods again. Gulls cross stitch white and grey, waves
collapse. Like me, they retreat and regroup. I will not grieve.
I have no more mourning left in me. Adept at swaddling
myself in black, I have rehearsed the role of widow.
I am ready to step to center stage. Loss of our three children

did not dam your poems, only release gates. I might have
forgiven you if words didn't continue to pour. Writing for you
was everything. After each birth was followed by another death,
I despaired, but you'd quote, *If Winter comes, can Spring
be far behind?* For you, April was the body of another woman.
Now that you're dead, your poetry will provide money, support,
I never had from you in life. Percy Florence and I will never buy
stale bread or hide from the butcher again. After your corpse

drifts ashore, I will burn you, heart and all, place your ashes
in Rome's Protestant Cemetery near your *Willmouse* because
for once, you didn't leave, stayed in the library with his coffin.
I wonder—would you have preferred to be buried nearer Keats
than your own son? If it is still in your pocket, I will save
Keats's volume of 1820 you always carried. Will it be open
to *La Belle Dame sans Merci*, the poem you read aloud
when you wanted to taunt me? If my heart were a granary,

I'd store such hurts but out of necessity, your words will
be *winged seeds* I can hinge on my back to carry me

through my future and fulfill your plea to the West Wind:
*Scatter, as from an unextinguished hearth / Ashes
and sparks, my words among mankind!* Heat from fire
you kindled that I will soon reflect to others may in time
ignite my heart, but I will never allow it to consume me again.
What I don't feel today is guilt. I learned about the word

early, knowing my mother, Mary Wollstonecraft, died
from childbed fever as a result of my birth. Her daughter,
I suckled on *A Vindication of the Rights of Woman* until
you came to sit at the feet of fame, to worship my father,
William Godwin, in the charmed circle I was banished
from at fourteen. Because my step-mother found me trying,
a handful, I was farmed out to Dundee, Scotland to live
with the Baxter family. After two years, I was allowed

to return to my father who was my God. To make you
notice me on your second visit to our house in London,
I chose words as if they were snowdrops I had picked
to mark early spring by making a bouquet. You invited
me to go for a ride, and pointed at the mare harnessed
to your carriage to show me *proud flesh,* a name for scars
on a horse where skin grows back across a wound.
Because it has been tested, flesh underneath is stronger

than the original. Buttoning my dress, smoothing my hair,
we returned to my father. At sixteen, I did not understand
your vocabulary lesson. Today, at twenty-four, I do. My
heart has its reasons, Percy; whip marks must be forgiven,
must be forgotten if they are to heal. Before a funeral pyre
is lit, I will dislodge your ring for our son Percy Florence,
and in time, I may even teach him to believe in its motto,
that the good time will come: *Il buon tempo verra.*

READING: POET LAUREATE OF CONNECTICUT

—For Charlotte Mew, 1867–1928

Eeling in the back of R. J. Julia's Booksellers because my socks
don't match, I head for the cushioned seat under the bay window
so I can tuck my feet up. It's August, my face is pale as a tulip
bulb, but next week, I'll *stalk*, Alida Monro's description of you
entering her Poetry Bookshop. Voice narrowing to a wire when
asked if, in fact, you were Charlotte Mew, you answered, *I am*

sorry to say I am. My signature's not painted on R. J. Julia's
wood floors like other poets; I mutter your line*: To the larks that
cannot praise us, knowing nothing of what we do.* Here with me,
helmeted in felt pork-pie hat, head cocked, Charlotte, you would
unfurl a horn-handled umbrella held under your arm, not to ward
off rain congealing to Bloomsbury pudding, but to defy Volvos,

BMWs curbed on US 1 in Madison. A rough-edged shard, not
smooth as sea glass or the even tans at the Surf Club, you had no
enclave like Emily Dickinson or *A Room of One's Own* upstairs
in R. J. Julia's loft. No retreat from caring, a mother who made
you starch curtains, stitch covers for chairs. No white dress, you
had coal to haul, floors and clothes to scrub. Asylumed for life,

faces of younger sister and brother imprinted by your daily visits
held you to a vow of chastity. I picture you writing novels,
heartfelt, but stilted, seen by your other sister, Anne, so hungry
she thumbs motes of cracker into her mouth. Almost fifty
before you published your first book, *The Farmer's Bride*,
in 1916, with lines in *the sweet-briar air* that lift me like wings

of a monarch, your words the pollen gilding my fingers. You cut
off hope of love, though not the ache. Did Thomas Hardy copy
Fin de Fête on a British Museum Reading Room slip because

the poem was for him? At the burial of his ashes in Westminster
Abbey, surely you whispered, *Sweetheart, for such a day/ One
mustn't grudge the score;/ Here, then, it's all to pay, / It's Good-*

night at the door. Woven or caught in a braid of love, darkness
grew like a cataract filming your eyes. A life you could not shed
like skin: a nursing home in Beaumont Street with no outlook,
the room in back, a high grey brick wall blocking sunlight, stars.
With only occasional pigeons as company, you longed for a visit
from anyone, even men picking up trash. Lost, you were useless

as nets beaten into a frazzle, frayed by mussel shells and clogged
with seaweed. Through a gauze of over seventy years, Charlotte,
life looks softer removed from the mesh of a real body. Even ink
has faded on the death certificate that says you died by your own
hand *while of unsound mind* on March 23, 1928. So many years
of cleaning, your hands were numb, but not your throat when

Lysol, a comet shooting through you, left a tail of pain curling
like a tongue, licking at what would soon no longer be there.
In coves of Long Island Sound, who can say why a place resists
freezing. Undercurrents, perhaps, like ones in "Fame": *A blot
upon the night,/ The moon's dropped child!,* lines that punctuate
like periods or the Thimble Islands lining Connecticut's coast.

Life should not be a test of what can be endured, what can be
survived. Outside the door of Alida Monro's bookstore, the thud
of the gold beaters hammering rang in your ears. Sixty poems
you left keep their rhythm in my heart, keep it beating steady
as oars rowing near a glacier with waves breaking on its flanks,
the deceiving sound of shoreline when there is no shore.

DOLL: PAPUSZA, GI JOE, BARBIE, MADAME ALEXANDER

In 1949, I told Jerzy Ficowski, if you print my songs in *Problemy*,
my people will be naked, I will be skinned alive. Ficowski
used my real name, Bronislawa Wajs, even though I'm known

by my gypsy name, Papusza, which translates to doll. Desperate
to reclaim my ideas, my words, I rushed to Warsaw, begged
the Polish Writer's Union to intervene. At the publishing house,

no one understood me. I went home, burned all of my work,
three hundred poems. That did not matter to the Baro Shero,
I was *magerdi*, defiled. Punishment was irreversible: exclusion.

It's raining again, a cold prickly rain that makes the window
look like a Spielberg effect on TV. If only my memories could
dissolve one luminous dot at a time but the mud season has

begun with snowmelt. The mantle of the earth is mush, sucking
off my boots when I try to walk away. Water stains spread out
on the ceiling like an antique map of my heart. Thirty-four years,

alone, shunned by nieces, nephews, unknown to their children,
I'm discarded, mute as my name, Doll. My family's voice, I still
hear it in my voice which is my mother's, my father's voice.

The older I have gotten, the more I recall although I will allow
no one to listen to my poems or songs. Harpists, my people
hauled great stringed instruments upright as if they were sails

on wagons carting us from northern Lithuania to eastern Tatras.
If we stopped for more than a day, I'd steal a chicken, take it
to another villager to exchange for reading and writing lessons.

Another chicken or two, I got a book or paper. When my father or
    brothers caught me, I was beaten, my books, poems buried.
    Married at fifteen to Dionizy Wajs, revered as a harpist but old,

I had a work station in a courtyard corner, a tin tub on wood. Pour
in boiling water: rub, rub, rub. The rhythm in my poems was born
in blankets and rugs, the words in my unhappiness.

I was the youngest wife, a *boria*, who got up before everything even
the *khaxni,* the hens. In the sooty light, I followed the rules: move
in silence, collect wood, build the fire, heat water, coffee,

do not speak to a man in the morning before he washes his face.
All day I talked about sheep parts: brains, balls, guts, organs,
glands, skinned heads, joints. I would pinch other girls' breasts

in greeting, in play. None of my hard work was mentioned when I
was pronounced *magerdi* and then banished from the *kumpani.* The
charges spoken were that I had no children, that I invented

long ballads to lament being poor, impossible love, rootlessness,
lost freedom and the *lungo drom,* or long road. A gypsy, I had
ou topos, no place to dream about, no homeland to yearn for.

Tinsmiths, blacksmiths but no Romulus and Remus, no Aeneas
wandering to do battle for me. No anthem or Holocaust memorial
because no names were recorded. Bronislawa Wajs, I sang poems

in Romani called the cant of thieves, argot of liars, but changing
words meant survival depending on secret laws that could never
be written in order to hide the past, to make a hedge to protect us

from the *gadje,* the non-Gypsies. I blackened pages with elegies for
our nomadic life spread out like skeletons of carp stretched
on a map of Europe. For thirty-four years, I have hidden my face,

114

afraid to thumb books or open newspapers, see Ficowski's face
who'll ask *So now where is your poetry?* Silenced by exclusion,
living in a well, no voice called down, Papusza. Romani echoes.

Marime, Magerdi is still warm as the spot where Baro Shero
touched the finger I had used to write down our gypsy songs.
Sentient, my hands kept memory, could not let go, could not ball

to a fist, penetrate the hedge. Bronislawa Wajs will be closed
over; *death date unknown* will be my final sentence. I told Jerzy
Ficowski, if you print my songs, my people will be naked, I will

be skinned alive. My words did not ignite even a tiny flicker,
but mouth to my ear, voices I remember that will be buried with
me have more than the sound of one lifetime, more than my own.

EVE'S STORY, REVISED

I. Eve, Flashing Her Key

No snailing into the Frederick Lewis Allen Memorial Room,
Eve barrels the main entrance of the New York Public Library,

past stairs to double doors of darkening mahogany. Forbidding,
no lettering identifies them, but Eve has latched the brass ring,

the charm, the talisman. Imagine what she will have: a desk,
leather books, manuscripts she saw on class day in the Beinecke.

Daylight fades the marble and wood panels that surround a space
with eleven cubicles for writers. Eve picks the second row, third

from the right, inserts hair sprayed bouffant, standard as WWI
helmets. Female, she doesn't have a scientific mind, her eye isn't

on a microscope, but a cart inside the door. Betty Friedan picks
up books, discards pink slips, lowers herself behind a partition

to write *Feminine Mystique*. Susan Brownmiller's striped socks
stick out over a chair. Eve watches her small feet curl and uncurl

writing *Against Our Will*. Everyone's quiet, careful not to disturb
manuscripts piled, vertebrae in the spine of the future. Hungry,

Eve goes to a cafeteria, chews while Nancy Milford plots *Zelda*.
Expert in domestic conflict, she irons issues Theodore H. White

has crafting *Making of the President: 1964*. Asked what she'll
write, Eve speaks of spontaneous erosion of a fossil that comes

from grating Parmesan each day, fighting with wine for reason,
of renting patent shoes. Advising Joseph Lash on *Eleanor and*

Franklin, she explains how a body can become grain rising from
wood, shows him how much power is in a woman's balled fist.

Eve tells Lash to experiment: hold a smile, be silent for an hour,
teeth clenched, a ventriloquist who never permits her lips to part

II. Her Name Said It All

Arriving a little late, Eve would shrink into her desk outside
the horseshoe I had formed, complaining that my class reminded
her of a Quaker meeting. When she'd had as much silence as she
could take, she'd answer questions. At break, Eve ate oranges,

fingering the peel like Braille or a palm reader unable to predict
her own future. I had stored my poems on a disk, turning from
words that flattened injustice, unwilling to file genital mutilation
under *G,* rape under *R.* I was a woman of action, pictured Eve

barging up the river. My engine pumping, I'd be a tugboat who
pushed her. Uncooperative, Eve told me I talked on the phone
too much, slept too much. She took valium in class, dropped
notes more than once, told me she drove away from a Mercedes

she'd backed into at Marshalls, leaving no note, how she'd steal
metaphors for poems because she had so little time. Eve wanted
to say too much, too fast. She let me know her arrows pointed
one way, wrote about yearning for a night of passion that would

stay, a moon floating in morning sky. Like having laser surgery
in Boston, her vision cleared. She filled pages about Fair Haven,
looking out her window at the wrong time when a boy's body
was being carried out, teaching the neighbor's girl how to bite,

being careful not to disrupt the alignment of her teeth. Eve tied
roses by stems, hung them upside down, labeling the bouquets:
Mussolini, His Mistress. When wind blew in the right direction,
air Eve breathed was porgy, sticky, old as flypaper. Sunlight

in corn silk will remind me of her hair, ground pesto her hands.
She taught me to make hollyhock ladies: select onion-dome buds
for heads because they'd stay closed; for the skirts, pinch off
half-open blossoms, the ones whose future was the least certain.

III. Eve Plans Her Funeral

Whiffenpoofs will assemble with their glasses raised
    on high to toast her final exit from Mory's,
wipe the last of the green, then the brown velvet

cup from her head. No *Amazing Grace* rising out
    of white Methodist clapboard outside Cecelia,
Kentucky and seven people around a hillside grave,

Eve will be a Townshend, live in the tan Victorian
    that overlooks all of New Haven Harbor.
An organ will swell Battel Chapel with fight songs,

Bulldog, Bulldog, Bow, Wow, Wow. If she had
    quarterbacked Yale's victory over Harvard in '39,
when Japanese planes attacked Pearl Harbor, Eve

would have been urged to fight on the football field.
    One old blue after another would detail how in 1942
with guns blazing, gas rationing and travel limitations

the order of the day, Eve came from behind with
    her spectacular arm, arcing a pass that covered
seventy yards. That was the game winning score; Eve

was the star. At the end of her memorial, voices will
  swell, *For God, for Country and for Yale.* Pulling
rabbits from a hat, one after another, hands twined

with ivy will tug out white handkerchiefs and wave
  them in the air. Balconies will overflow to flood
the dinosaur room in the Peabody Museum, elbow

pressed to elbow around the brontosaurus. Grief will
  not melt like mozzarella over ziti in tin foil trays;
blackened salmon hors d'oeuvres will blot every eye.

IV. Eve's Obituary for the New Haven Garden Club

An iris hurling to sun, bearded for stately elegance,
Eve's rhizome stayed at soil level. Cultivating shallowly
because roots were on surface, she practiced good horticulture,
never planted before mid-October. Eve did not know cancer

cells could spread, like tubers lumping, rising in soil, pushing
through as if bone from skin. First, for the Spring Show,
Eve planted *Bride's Halo*, pristine, white satiny petals
bordered with a narrow gold halo, flowers frilled and lightly

laciniated. Next, there was *Ecstatic Echo*, with light orchid
fading to white, rich coppery-red falls and bright yellow beards.
To celebrate her first wedding anniversary, Eve planted
Champagne Elegance, apricot amoeba, ruffled falls of buff,

avocado and peach. Hidden, bruises began to rival purple
Dusky Challenger and deep violet peppering plicates
of *Jessie's Song.* Eve wanted to fill every club member's hands
with coral pink of *Beverly Sills,* but it was the apricot of

Wayside Sunset that strung the diamond and pearl women
of Old Orchard Road out into early evening light. No, Eve
didn't miss traveling. She planted *Victoria Falls* with Yale blue
and white patches. To keep the playing field level, she added

the vibrant Harvard crimson of *Sultan's Palace*. There was
Hawaiian Serenade to add a taste of peach, tangerine, lavender,
Pride of Ireland for green touched with darker green. Before
she was cast out for doing her own composting, Eve put

in bed after bed of pink colored *Paradis*, iridescent Tiffany.
No carnival glass for her. Bedding iris on the south side
of her Fair Haven house, she knew what color each clump
would lift, piled white on white. Eve would not compromise,

wanted tubers overflowing one bucket, then another. Aging,
she didn't care if it was the season to dig or reset. Unable to wait,
her fingers wove in and over soil to separate roots. Streaked by
beading sweat, she dug up the old rhizome too dense for bloom.

V. This Is What Desire Looks Like Unconsummated

How can a person be buried with so much music inside?
Treble notes bound along to the left of bass, rising
from ink spots in the score. Wipe pages clean, notes

will be blackbirds swallowed whole. Eve, you watched
through chain link fence as your neighbor and his son fought.
Knowing how important it was to say what had to be said,

you told our workshop about your husband cradling you
before last sips of whiskey. Tipping a square bottle neck
to his lips, angry, he talked with his fists, splitting eyebrows,

your mouth. In January, when even the Quinnipiac River
was scaled in ice, only the weather grew sober. Stars
in the water were tarnished by oil spill, like the quarters

that were all you had to throw into St. Mary's collection plate.
A corpse with hair that refused to curl, a face without rouge
or lipstick, you are shut up inside mahogany costing more

than anything you ever owned in life. Edging along the streets
of Fair Haven, each footstep behind you like a razor edge
to your throat, your poems were the scream you didn't make

when your purse was snatched. Listening for a harbor bell,
by the time you took a seat in my class, put words onto a page,
it was too late. You were too old and the cancer had already

begun. No arm of a river muscling into Long Island Sound,
you were bobbing too far out to drift back as wood will do.
Eve, you taught me beach plum jam, pressing rose hips

for scurvy tea, digging for cherrystones. Pointing out black
Adidas sneakers over phone wires that marked Latin King
territory, you mimed a mouth opening and waiting for crack

to kick in, how to palm the glass vials. Teasing tied pit bulls,
you wanted sudden death, not cancer, but the bullet that strayed
into a seven-month-old boy in his crib next door to your house.

MONROE: SWEETHEART OF THE MONTH

Curious, really, that something was perfectly
made, outrageous actually in its regularity:
breasts, waist, thighs, calves, ankles. Nested
in red velvet, clothing removed, not even
a wig, refusing to wear anything that was not
God's gift, you warmed hands between legs
as the photographer, Tom Kelley, begged,
Marilyn, baby, act surprised, act ashamed.

Right at the start, you might have thought
your body was what a calendar manufacturer
was after, but posing was not just a matter
of changing feet. There had to be no more
chilling rarity. Pinching back of your neck
to stay awake, did you think of hot cloths
for starched lips? Set by the camera, weight
will not mock you, *Playboy*'s first centerfold.
December, 1953. That first issue was undated
to ride the newsstands as long as possible.

Seventy thousand copies sold to hands lifted
as if in blessing, then lowered to smooth out
the creases again and again on your picture:
Golden Dreams, worn like a saint's medallion
on belt buckles or a communion wafer on
a thrusting tongue. Marilyn, not knowing how
to get by on what came along—Clark Gable
saying, *She made a man proud to be a man,*
in *The Misfits,* your last film—did you think
of black under Tom Kelley's camera cloak, or
being covered by sheets you had not explored?

Metamorphoses

I. Revising the Canon: A Stag Party

Too much light to sleep. At ease, Actaeon and his men
dripped in blood hunted hot, burning. Inlet shade, Diana

bathed with Crocale and Hephele, arms unsheathed.
Only the sea was fertile, no other fluids caressed. Odor

of shellfish, open mussels, the gills of a fish whose fins
brushed their breasts, sweet as a tongue flicking nipples.

Hollowed by the women's heels, holes foamed as thighs
were pushed apart. Receding waves sucked, melted

buttocks that skinned rhythms on sand as yet not tracked
by any man. Each lathering the other—knees, shoulders,

navels and backs—fingers snaked, probed, then spread lips
to water, wet, warm as a woman's mouth. Brown strands

of unbound hair wove into seaweed wrapping calves. No
thrust, only licking then curling. Nothing hard until Hephele

glanced at Actaeon, stilled, above them. Diana reddened,
resentful of this pleasure cheaply gained. Having no weapon,

she let words fly: *Boast if you can that you have seen Diana
naked.* This chance but crucial junction shocked marrow

in his bones. As inner and outer self merged, horns grew.
Words froze in his throat like lard at the baying of Harpy

and Tigress, independent bitches who picked out which
of the hounds they would service in the pack. Air filled

with teeth; Actaeon moaned as the dogs snarled. Now, he
was the one ripped open, pressed down, legs apart with no

escape. One bitch stripped his flank; another tore his head.
Some thought Diana merciless, others praised her sentence.

II. Scientific Knives Are Sharp, Not Mythical

When Iphis forced her way from womb to day,
Telethusa could picture her new daughter
with breasts rolling in small mounds. Lidgus

had fathered her saying, *If it should be a girl,*
throttle her, drown her like a cat. Saving
her hands to knead bread, Telethusa told Ligdus

he had a son. Thirteen years of balancing without
a pole, wishing she was a real man, Iphis trembled
while straddling Ianthe, unable to fulfill her desire,

If only Iphis' father had valued women more.
Lessons were learned in biology. Reassured
by classroom rote, Iphis chose a plastic surgeon

with enameled facts to be her god. Trans-sexual
operations were an anatomy lesson in pink or blue,
but not a slight procedure: breasts flattened, nipples

remained, labia sewn shut, lumps and a roll
of flesh added. Prick the skin and hormones passed.
Up through half-light to day, an empty elevator

clanged its doors, a bare stretcher trembled. No
one sang her song, held rattles or torches. Iphis
had three legs at last and rising on two of them,

made way to a toilet where mortal coils distilled
a drop. The doctor proudly unwrapped his wedding
gift for Ianthe. Finally, Iphis was his father's son.

III. Daphne and Apollo

Daphne was another independent love and marriage
hating young huntress and no wonder. Women one
after the other had either aborted, lost their names
or gassed themselves in the long procession. The most
Daphne might expect was to drag from state to state
packing, unpacking, papering bathroom walls in tigers.
She wrote couplets, sang them to every man she met:

If men were golden rods growing,
women would get scythes for mowing.

If men were trout in water clear,
smart women would grab a sharp spear.

If men like deer on hills did run,
women would learn to shoot a gun.

A hound startling a rabbit, Apollo ran for game, Daphne
safety. Worn out, a victim to long flight, her limbs grew
numb, heavy, rooted to the ground. Hair pruned, she
woodenly kissed Apollo and wreathed his head, a laurel.

IV. *New Haven Register's* **Symphony Supplement:**
   Mrs. Jove Models Latest Fur

Io tightened sheets stretched through her thighs
as oak limbs, or what she hoped were branches

and not tips of horns, scraped her window. Only
leaves breathed as Jove hoofed the screen, climbed

through. Enter and stroke. Pull then release. Pause
only for a final contraction. A jet of milk ringing

into a pail, Jove foamed. White, shiny as a heifer, Io
became his bride, finger wreathed in gold, diamonds,

not in a brass ring like any common cow's nose.
She was licensed and then recorded under Jove.

Chain linked in a pasture, beleaguered by gadflies,
milk cows can grow too old to freshen. Shopping

for cruise wear, Io drove her Range Rover from Saks
to Lucy Baltzell's, then Nora Zandre's. No T. J. Maxx

or Marshall's for Jove's wife. Io volunteered, played
tennis, did speed training with a personal trainer, got

a pedicure every day. Getting through meals of pasta,
sauce on the side, Prozac didn't silence lowing that filled

her throat. Fingering dust on the piano the new maid
had left, she engraved an *I* and *O,* then wiped it clean.

V. Pygmalion and Galatea

One man, Pygmalion, had seen shameful women
leading lives as surgeons slicing male genitals
or perfecting a uterus that snapped in and out.
He was shocked at their vices: females cursed,

kept their own names, gave birth alone to children,
did not scrub toilets. Pygmalion knew that nature
had given women wombs and breasts as armor
for motherhood, no more. He lived alone, placed

no one in his bed until he found a girl like a piece
of unchiseled marble. Skilled as Pygmalion was
in the art of concealing art, he carefully molded
and named her, Galatea. Loving ways he could play

with his workmanship, his doll, he tucked Galatea
in bed at night, but not before spreading her legs.
Mounted like a hobby horse, she made no sound,
not even MaMa or DaDa. Wax made pliable

by handling grows soft. Galatea started to change
at Pygmalion's touch: nipples would rise, veins
throbbed under his thumb, her breath quickened
almost as if a goddess had intervened. In a rainbow

after a storm, colors blend. The eye cannot detect
a line, yet the arcs are altogether different.
Pygmalion could not define a boundary Galatea
had crossed, but she was not humble in his presence.

Grafted, twigs knit and mature. Galatea was filled
with blooms, an apple tree with promise. Refusing
a harvest, Pygmalion's passion waned as frost does
dissolving over crocus in an early spring morning.

VI. Brueghel's Icarus: An Old Husband's Tale

how it takes place/ While someone else is eating
    —W. H. Auden

Daedalus was not a man, Icarus no boy. That's a myth.
Without a husband to bind her, Daedalus turned nature
inside out, taught her daughter to fly from earth; after all,

men couldn't fence air. Feathering Icarus in sequence
as a pan pipe rises, Daedalus twined quills to mold two sets
of wings sealed in an icing of white wax, stiff as bridal lace.

Daedalus hovered, warning: *Keep mid-way; water weights*
and sun burns. Always follow me. Icarus rose or was pulled
up, casting her shadow on a ploughman, head lifted from

his rut, who grumbled, *A woman's place is in the home.*
The mother tried to lift her arms higher to buffer her daughter
but blue enveloped Icarus who cried, *Let's fly all the way*

to Trinacria. Knowing Samos was north and Calymne east,
Icarus ignored the earth's warning being traced out for her
by the sharded coast of Crete. Filial duty cannot blot desire

as the moon eclipses the sun. Perhaps there was a brilliance
gleaming in Icarus' green eyes that flashed, mercifully
blocking the sight for Daedalus: her only child encircling

wings, writhing like a corn snake carried aloft by a hawk.
Imagine the girl, her mother's support failing, the aerial lift
and impulse spent. Dripping to the sea, only wax hissed,

floating like islands seem to do. Daedalus did not fly again.
Unused, feathers yellowed; wax stiffened in her wings
that stretched out more like a shroud than a swan in flight.

VII. Arethusa Speaks to Alpheus as He Pursues Her

With his magical spell he taught a river to dive.
   —Moschus

You offer this shaft as something I could use.
   The shape is handsome and unmarked as a new
   mushroom, I will admit. Responsive, intelligent,
you say. I could teach it to perform, stand upright

on command, then come and fetch me strings
   of lapis, azure or even gold. A tent on your pole,
   my labia could fold, take your shape, rising moist
as pliable canvas, filling like a sail on the mast

of a ship. My mouth around it would say
   only that like the sea, your staff lacks perfume,
   tastes of salt. There must be some talent to raise
it high above the ordinary. Does it sing?

Though the shape is very suggestive, I cannot
   find a use for it, even to stir my soups, or pen poems
   but I will keep my left hand in your pant pocket
for one week, if I must, and learn your ebb

and flow. Now your flesh seems tame enough
   while I stroke it, limp as a tired fish, slightly damp.
   Good God! It moves. Who trained it to live erect
and hard without air, without warmth or a home?

Still, it continues to grow like a prickly pear cactus.
   Will it bloom for only one night like the cereus?
   I think I should tell you that I have two deft hands,
plenty for my need. You might take their place.

I ask only that you never climb in bed, slide
    under cover and grab my genitals like a blind limb
    thrusting toward heat. You should begin at the top
of my throat on my lips, treacherous from solitude

that has taught me how to shape and speak empty
    promises to other men. Become a stream, make
    your way far under bushes, dive deep in my tunnel,
mingle your water with mine. Let the fountain spray!

The Statue, *The Death of Cleopatra*, Speaks to Me in The National Museum of American Art

I.

I notice you are taken captive by the size, articulation
and muscles of my hands and not my bared right breast.
My sculptor, Edmonia Lewis, held up her black palm
to my white one, making our fingers match. Without her,
I might have been a slab hauled by men with dirt caked nails
to a grand hotel lobby in Rome to top a Victorian table.

Instead, here I sit, a shrine enthroned in my own room—
Edmonia's 1.5-ton tombstone of winter white marble.
Your brochure says she was born in Greenbush, N.Y.
in about 1844. Finally, in 2018, a death notice: 9/17/1907
in London. An unmarked grave, she knew I'd be her voice.
Edmonia's father was West Indian, her mother was part

Chippewa. Orphaned early, she may have been raised
by her mother's tribe. You can begin to see the problem
the curator had preparing the brochure you're scribbling on.
In 1859, Edmonia attended Oberlin College, learned to draw.
Maybe it was her color, perhaps her talent that motivated
two white classmates to accuse her of poisoning their lunch,

and cause them to lose a competition she won. Believe me,
I could have taught her a thing or two about using poison.
Since it's an understatement to call my family dysfunctional,
I always carried poison in a hollow comb. Somewhat painful
for me to do, I had to test it first on slaves so the timely death
of my sister seemed natural. Don't go jumping to conclusions.

It's pure speculation that I pushed my younger brother
Ptolemy into the Nile in a full suit of golden armor—
I was too frugal. Perhaps because she was poor, Edmonia
was more passive than I would have been. While awaiting
arraignment in Oberlin, she was abducted by a white
mob and beaten, prompting an Ohio judge to drop charges

of poisoning her classmates. Grateful it was ribs, not fingers
that were broken, afraid to return to school, she went
to Boston and then to Rome. I would have told her to wear
silk pants tight as cherry skins, not mannish clothes—rakish
red cap, burgundy shawl big as a tent or when sculpting,
a brown tweed jacket fit for a camel. Yes, I will admit to you

that I was dramatic, craved attention, went a little over the top
while decorating my barge for my first meeting with Anthony:
silver oars, purple sails, flutes, harps, jasmine perfume fanned
into air by my half naked slaves. I was Venus in gold brocade
waiting to be unwrapped under a canopy splattered in stars.
Who could have resisted this body? Only the guard keeps men

who stand where you are off my thighs. I was a block of marble
that begged Edmonia for revelation, and in her hands stone
moved like clouds reshaping in wind. Others had sculpted
my real life beauty, contemplation of suicide, but she chose
to carve me right after last breath, catch tension of balance
between repose and gravity of death. It is the angles Edmonia

created: ankle, knee, hip and neck bent back, yet just forward
enough to show I was still yearning for Anthony's touch.
William Wetmore Story—you know the one immortalized
in Hawthorne's *The Marble Faun*—had carved me. Benchmark
for sculpture, I was calm, regal, and ideal—the three words I
would never use about myself. Neo-classical, an aristocrat

of the male canon, Story was afraid of emotion, would never
have given his life to be consumed by passion. Grouping
Edmonia in *a set whom I do not like*, Story did not have
Edmonia's dreams of being beaten by white hands raised
over her black head that lifted her from sleep each night.
An ache in five ribs that never quite healed gave her reason

to avoid symmetry she had not found in past life. Say, can
you stop taking notes long enough to look up to admire how
my neck is elongated so my head rests on the throne's edge
in order to emphasize my profile? My left hand, cuffed
in gold at the wrist, hangs off its arm as if weighted by stone.
A bracelet above my right elbow, my fingers curl on my knee.

Coiled, the asp rests its head on my thumb. Small, reed thin,
no more than a foot long, the snake shed no drop of blood
as signature. Leaving no trail, it shrouded my body in mystery
that still exists about Edmonia's death and burial. Setting out
every day, determined to honor the world of artists like Story
who didn't respect her, she kept people at a distance. Her need

in a fist, there was tenderness in her words: *I have a strong
sympathy for all women who have struggled and suffered.*
Carving her own marble because male sculptors would have
claimed the work was created by native stonecutters, she used
a blackboard to sketch with chalk, but nothing fully existed
for her until it was tested by palms, fingertips. Tap, tap, tap

became music sweeter to me than flutes seaming heavy air
above the Nile. So skilled her hands appeared absent minded,
she let them wander all over me until I could Braille her pulse.
Chipping then polishing, Edmonia would ask me what was
the sense in having dreams, would heaven continue to feed
her hunger, encourage hope that drains the heart? Often short

133

of breath from sting of marble dust on her tongue, in her nose
and throat, she'd sit tucking her knees into bent elbows, trying
to make her body very small. Each day now, remembering how
she fumbled in a pocket for tissue, I know there's no need
to watch for the daughter or son Edmonia yearned for to enter.
I'd like to think she chiseled, then carved me out of her womb.

II.

Headlines from Philadelphia's 1876 Centennial Exposition
and Chicago's 1878 Interstate Industrial Exposition read:
Edmonia Lewis and Her Statue, Cleopatra: Stars. Even so,

unable to sell me and too poor to ship two tons of marble
to Rome, Edmonia put me in storage. We didn't stay in touch.
A card in the museum table you are leaning on says all that's

known about her final years is that she lived in Rome until
1907. Let me tell you, my last years as a statue sure were public.
By 1892, I was front and center in a Clark Street Chicago saloon.

On a bet, gambler and racehorse owner, "Blind John" Condon
mounted me on the grave of his favorite horse—you guessed it—
Cleopatra. I guess being a tombstone in front of the grandstand

at his Harlem Race Track west of the Windy City was no more
humiliating than rolling myself in bedding and being delivered
as merchandise to Caesar who was into his fifties and balding.

"Blind John" also appreciated beauty—a covenant in his deed
required me to stay on the property. Indignity was heaped upon
indignity. I'll confess, nothing humiliated me like Octavia did,

parading an effigy of me, arms wreathed in gold snakes through
Rome. The racetrack became a golf course, then a WWII
torpedo factory. Do you golf? Well, be careful when you tee off.

Those balls were murder—knocked off my nose, half my chin!
Eighty years later, a mailing site was built; in 1972, a contractor
hauled me to a Cicero storage yard. Acid rain on the golf course

abraded my marble's surface to sugar. Blue cleaning liquid used
on my head and breasts after saloon fights left deep stains. It's
easy to see you know getting old is tough, about rolling off bar

stools. Finally, over a hundred years later, I was news again.
The *Chicago Tribune* reported a fire inspector, Harold Adams,
spotted me in Cicero, said I *was like a big white ghost lying*

out there between all that heavy machinery and crying out
to be saved. To earn badges, his son's Boy Scout troop cleaned
me so I'd *look decent until somebody came along who'd know*

better what to do. Sure, it was nice to have young boys probing
every inch of me, but then they sprayed on layers of white paint,
stored me in Forest Park shopping mall avalanched in discarded

Christmas garland, Thanksgiving turkeys, pumpkins, and rabbits.
Reclaimed in 1994 for the National Museum of American Art,
I was a poster child for plastic surgery. On my right hand, asp

and fingers replaced, nose, chin, and headdress reconstructed,
sandals were restored to feet. At last, Edmonia and I are stars,
back in the spotlight where we belong. Don't you think I'm still

regal, a commanding presence? Never treated like royalty,
all her life, Edmonia fought being labeled African-American
or Native-American by men like Henry James who mocked her

sisterhood, called her *a negress, whose colour picturesquely*
contrasting with that of her plastic material, was the pleading
agent of her fame. If her grave were found and marked today,

the tombstone would have no hyphen, one title: *SCULPTOR.*

III.

Edmonia knew what stirs underneath a skirt. Even in death,
more than a hint of heat seeps out of my pores: oil of rose,
honeysuckle, and lavender in every crevice, even soles
of my feet. Does your ordinary heart ever stumble? Have you
known how when the heartbeat doubles, night can quicken?
Suffice it to say that Anthony never tried to comprehend

the black hole of existence, even though I pried understanding
out of each day. A blaze of blood asserting right of way,
entering me like a sharp intake of breath, only sleep drained
him from my body. Your smile shows you do understand men.
Yes, at first it was lust. Then I couldn't put a name to hunger
that bound us. There were promises and lies; there was darkness;

but there were dreams for our children. Drinking and gambling,
we'd dress as servants and roam streets taunting my subjects.
Even wind seemed to gossip about us down dung filled streets.
Thinking of Anthony getting up to speak at an all-night party
but throwing up instead in the skirt of his toga held by a friend,
I couldn't understand why John Dryden complained Anthony

was *unbent, unsinewed, made a woman's toy.* Like Dryden,
a man, Shakespeare got it all wrong. I didn't try to stab a courier
who brought news of Anthony's marriage to Octavia. I knew
a political move when I saw one. After our reunion in Antioch,
I had Anthony's son, our third child, and as you must know,
good day care was hard to come by, what with my relatives

lurking in the halls. With four children, I had no time to loll
for hours in ass's milk or drink pearls dissolved in vinegar—
for one thing, that doesn't work and I'd never waste good pearls.
Do you have any idea how many hours I spent trying to adjust

and lower taxes? Who remembers me doling out free grain in
hard times? Now, maybe the nipples on my bared breasts would

have made even a prune like Octavian gasp, but I never turned
air around me sick with desire—I was not into pollution,
worked to clean up our environment, sponsored bills to build
aqueducts. Taking five years off my age so I'd be a sex kitten
for Caesar, George Bernard Shaw forgot to mention I was
the first in my family to learn the Egyptian language. At least

Plutarch recorded that I spoke seven languages: *It was
a pleasure merely to hear the sound of her voice, with which,
like an instrument of many strings, she could pass from one
language to another.* By 31 B.C., Anthony and I were bottled
up in Actium by Octavian who was across the Ambracian Gulf.
The winner wrote the history. Octavian said I turned tail and ran:

I was a woman and afraid; Anthony, a dog after a bitch in heat.
I was no coward and neither was he. Anthony loved me,
offered to kill himself in exchange for my life and our children.
I moved my treasury to a mausoleum with fuel to burn it,
locked myself inside. I suppose Anthony thought I was dead.
Roman to the end, he disemboweled himself—it's trickier

than it looks—and it was just like him to botch whacking
out his guts. Hauled up like a steer through a window
of my mausoleum, he died in my arms. I began to dream
of death, how I would go with him tasting his various parts.
I dressed myself in silk, my slaves exchanged one favor
for another, got Octavian's henchmen to bring a basket of figs—

the rest, you might say, is history. Shadows arched the walls,
I felt pain, human I twitched as I watched the asp bite me.
How old are you? I was thirty-nine. God bless Plutarch for
writing, *her old charm, and the boldness of her youthful beauty*

had not wholly left her and, in spite of her present condition,
still sparkled from within. Of course, I did know a few things

about fixing myself up, wrote a popular book on cosmetics
with ingredients like burnt mice. Labeled the last major threat
to Rome for years, I'd rather be remembered as the last great
power of the Hellenistic world. You know, I could have ruled
half the known world and with my four children enthroned,
the whole thing. Practical, a woman, I would have brought peace

to the Mediterranean—the gods had sent me to earth to do that.
But then I met Anthony, my sweet, unsalvageable Anthony.
Ours were not small deaths that went unnoticed like Edmonia's.
But now, I sit here, her flag, though not one of surrender. She
held her hand up as a model for my white one, not to dramatize
her blackness but to lift a voice against darkness of the world.

IV

No Brothers to Ferry My Father

Stringbean is what I call my father as he sands walnut
he had cut, hauled to Lexington from the farm before

it was put up for auction. He won't bandanna his mouth
breathes in dust as if inhaling his father, his youth. My talks

with my mother are best while we are chopping onions,
arguing about leaving red potato peels on or off for salad.

But, for my father, I rehash our road trips: my two sisters
in the Chevy's backseat drawing a line on vinyl I dared

not cross; flashlighted road maps; banging pots to scare
black bears away from our tent in the Smoky Mountains.

Rambling on about burning slash piles, my father will not
discuss cancer blacklining bones, only smell of chainsaws,

of clearcuts in Kentucky, Tennessee. Whorls in the wood
he planes are the color of old honey in a saucer magnolia

hollowed by insects, but there's not a sliver, not a splinter
of sweetness there from him for me. Fingering the grain

as if he were taking the wood's pulse, my father lectures
me about tongue and groove, oil, how not one drop of stain

is needed for wood darkened by one hundred years that link
generations I can't dovetail. Set in his ways, my father

still believes a daughter carries only blood, can't stencil
Shipley on a tag to hang on grandsons who will pass it on.

Seeing his family name over a picture of the Hardin County
smokehouse on my book cover gives him no comfort. With

my father, I'm still just a *dag gone girl*. I can't create a word
to keep him from the dark, the cold, from what has no name.

My Son's Poem for His Grandfather

Your grave jackhammered into Kentucky limestone,
I sheet you in red clay. Her head veiled in snow,
my mother is marooned with age, with mourning.
When she whispers, *Todd*, as I help her up from

knees that have failed, the love I hear in my name
does not comfort me. It is arrowheads I remember,
pulling down a Hush Puppy box with bowed sides.
Grandpa, you explained each point. One for a bird

had a fine, small tip, the telltale sign. The next
with wide barb and flaring sides was for a deer
so it did not flee in pain. Knowing which shape
to pick, you killed fox and mink for pelts to sell,

shot doves or a turkey for supper. Because each
time I asked, your story was the same, I knew
it was true. Never tiring of lifting chipped flint
tissued over more flint, you would double back

to the spring thaw with you, Paul and Justus,
your older brothers, competing for arrowheads.
As corn seed bags lightened, your overalls sagged
when you filled pockets with stone. Sharp ones

poked holes; Paul walked behind winding in the tail
you dropped. Yesterday, I saw two barns, all that
is left of your farm, chewed a plug around back,
spit tobacco juice in the pond like you did. Palming

a sliver of rock, chinking from the kitchen chimney,
I splintered wood off the smokehouse where

you sat after supper, vaulted split railing around
the back field for an arrowhead I could call mine.

Digging dirt you plowed, I picked what might have
been a spear. Unchanging, Howe Valley and its hills
have waited eighty-five years to claim you, Grandpa.
Enduring, they call out to me as one they now own.

DEADBOLT

I am resisting talking to old men in Stop and Shop,
whispering how my father taught me about sex
from corn: the tassel on the top of the stalk, the male;
silk feathering from the ear, the female. I don't ask
these old men where their daughters are, why they

are still alive when my father is not. Why should I
bother to tell them how, when my father was here,
I did everything the same way, every day. What good
did it do to mix sausage in milk gravy to pour over
biscuits, break waxed beans into one-inch pieces,

crumble his cornbread in milk? I will not help a single
other old man by ripping off plastic bags for oranges.
I do, however, show restraint when I don't knee one
stooping for a banana. Picking at portabella mushrooms,
I remember caps and gills glowing in their own light.

My father named it foxfire, luminescent as lightning
bugs, lush as glowworms. Foxfire migrated like my life,
now Connecticut with Kentucky receding like Calumet's
white fences under airplane wings at BlueGrass Airport.
I could not close my father's coffin lid like a hymnal,

or *cling to that old rugged cross and exchange it one
day for a crown* of Howe Valley's rosebud. Even light
from water colored by bourbon did not ease the fire
of my father's passage for me. No spells against grief,
no incantation to block longing, I now delight in scaring

three old men in Stop and Shop away from the produce
section by chanting: *Belladonna, henbane, elderberry,*

145

nightshade. What's the point in telling the man humped
over discounted day-old chopped beef that if Daddy were
here, he would be wearing a straw hat, would not mutter

to clerks about prices. Angry as I am, I do draw the line
at tripping old men still able to wheel their carts, don't
remind them what waits just beyond the door. I will not
describe how my father would check locks, imagining
a hard twist, but no deadbolt could stop multiplication

of cells. He swallowed fear like a pill. Even though I want
to leave, I won't help an old man fish for change in pants
at the Quick Check. He can see my money is already in
my hand. I'm resisting talking to old men in Stop and Shop.
Their words will not take a small bite out of my sorrow.

If Winter Comes

—Percy Bysshe Shelley

Bent more like I am curling or playing shuffleboard,
I rake leaves with my fingers. Peonies that I dug
from the side garden of the house my father built
are beginning to sprout. Because I could not stay

for the month, which might stretch into the two or more
the doctor said it would take for my father to die,
I carried my parents, what I was able to suitcase
from their lives, to Connecticut. I tried to make a joke

of bringing boxes of peony tubers shrouded in dirt from
the bluegrass, telling my mother she could ground
her feet, wiggle toes in Kentucky soil. Always the rebel,
even in a Yankee state, Daddy would not surrender

to death. For three springs, he saw white, fuscia, pink,
dangling in mid-air from a window where I'd placed
his bed. I wanted him to die in my home held by smell,
love of my sons, my husband, my mother. I gave up.

When a night nurse at Hospice phoned, saying my name
like a question, I had the chance to be someone else.
No amnesia at three in the morning. His cover was
all I carried back home. If bedroom walls could return

my father's voice to me, I would nap, feet wrapped
in that beige cashmere throw. Daddy wanted to leave
some trace, more than a shoebox of cards, more than
these peonies he watched me plant. Their tubers, thicker

than his thumbs, root in my heart. I know I need to live
in the moment, not what I cannot hold again, his hand.
But like using a knife to flense blubber from a whale,
I cannot skin my dreams: my father fielding grounders

on leveled turf, teaching me the importance of following
through. I want to palm the past, close it into a fist, but
a picture of Daddy's elbow resting on a Ford pickup truck
window albums me: Riverfront Stadium, Paramount Pickle

Day, playing dominoes and Bump, hand puppets of fox,
the rabbit, my father scratching our retriever's back with
his bare feet. Not like him, for me each year Rough Creek
grew fainter. Like sand on its banks, like the cancer that

bored into my father's bones, nothing stays static. Today,
I have uncovered peonies, a part of his spring that I did save.
Five mounds of maroon stalks bookmark my father's story.
Already the third of April, I can see it is time for me to buy

new garden gloves, wire cages to surround the stems, control
what of life I can. When I can bundle an armful of peonies'
life that is left from my father in this earth, will Howe Valley,
those hills that cradle his body, still have a hold on me?

First Ice

Unlike my sorrow which has started to scab,
grass has not closed over this raw red

Kentucky clay. Over eight months now.
My father's plot is still unmarked, a rupture

in my heart that needs to find a name
to heal. I've come back to these hills to see

the communion altar the Ladies' Guild
built in Howe Valley Methodist Church

with my donation, to measure other stones
so Daddy's will not be the tallest. He avoided

standing out, showing off in life, and there
is no reason I can think of he should in death.

Marble I had chosen yesterday is too black,
too glossy; I'll have to go back in the morning

to Cheneyville, prove Mr. Crum was right,
that it's women who always change their minds.

What I want is a pint bottle of Wild Turkey,
a jelly glass, to sit in my cousin Sue's kitchen

and nip at Jim's country ham. Instead, to thank
Hansel Pile for putting a wreath on my father's

grave, I head out across Hardin County, a place
so religious even grapevines are tied to crosses.

Sure enough, I find pictures of Jesus, head
wrapped in thorns, cracked linoleum floors,

deviled eggs sprinkled with paprika. Minding
my manners, I admire trophies won by Hansel's

bulls, linger over the photograph of Sammy,
his Grand Champion at the Indiana Fair. Done

with the judge's ring, Hansel tells me his secret:
a donkey to lead cattle around, get them used

to a rope. No blue ribbons for the donkey.
All night every night, it walked and walked,

stupid, helpless, tethered as it was to one halter
then another. In winter, Hansel turned the donkey

out to pasture without food. I imagine its cracked
hooves, scraping at what was in frozen ground,

stumbling through February, monotony broken
by breath, a shadow moving from tuft to tuft.

The donkey knew its duty here, knew its worth,
knew its only chance for hay, corn. A small gray

memory, each spring it came back to the pen
as I do to Howe Valley, these hills, to my father.

Tied to reason, to its life, I think of the donkey,
of what we accept if we wear it long enough

like the rope hooked to the bull, like octagonal links
of a gold necklace I finger, like the weight of grief.

IN DUNKIN' DONUTS WITH MY MOTHER

What was I thinking when I took her with me
to drink hot macchiato? Seeing the price,
my mother asks if I'm the Queen of Sheba.
Waving my wildflower guide like a semaphore,
she points to a picture of young chicory leaves
that color Morgan Point's marsh. Tomorrow,
my mother will uproot and pot chicory stems
in my cellar, teach me to roast and grind roots
to stretch out coffee. She's proud of pinching
pennies I won't stoop to pick up, brags how
chicory got her through the morning when
the egg money ran out. To distract her, I ask
about growing up in Kentucky, being in love.
More chicory. Called *Blue Sailors*, the flower
sprang up where a maiden died waiting for her
love to return from the Pacific. Hard to transplant,
chicory made up its own mind like my father
whose eyes were wild, brave blue as the weed.
Always hungry for coffee, red-eye gravy, letting
her know he was coming from the barn to wash up
for breakfast, Daddy's whistle ribboned the wind.

ALICE IN THE LOOKING GLASS

I cannot teach you children
How to live.—If not you, who will?
  —James Merrill

There is a room with a mirror on one side and an object,
say, your mother or a picture of your mother, on the other
    wall. If you face the mirror, and if the walls are close
    together, you could step forward to your mother's

    likeness. Reaching back, you might touch her kneeling
    with a brush in hand by your toilet or dropping wads
of paper towels like a flower girl at a wedding as she stretches
her arm around your bedroom windows to wash them. It's easier

to look at your mother in a mirror than to describe what she
does to you. Remember, cylindrical, spherical, convex, concave,
    flat or wavy, reflected objects retain their spatial
    relationship. You become confused only if you forget,

    like that time you won the poetry recitation. You came
    home, head stuck up proud as a moccasin swimming
on top of the water. Your mother didn't even turn her head
to nod but continued pruning grapevines for wreaths she

twisted and sold at Berea College. Even if you are only two
feet apart, love's not simple like the congruence of faces.
    Cleaned, glass in your windows offers imperfections or
    becomes a channel for unaltered embodiment: your mother

    backing into the screen door with her hip or rubbing
    her forehead with the heel of her hand after doing
supper dishes. Washing your hands over and over won't erase
splotches like your mother's oil colored stains etched by acid

from suckering tomatoes. To forget, it's worth the price of
admission to fun houses with mirrors that distort then conjoin.
Picture playing Hearts. You hold up a fan of cards, allow them
to tilt into her view but hide your eyes, masking the need. For

your mother's approval, you play Go Fish. Partial images in
carnival mirrors confuse with artifacts of the mother you
want to create, a past you need to settle like using place holders
to seat guests at dinner. Square or round, silvered glass fuses

living into a cooking lesson on TV which loses smell of garlic
cloves and basil leaves scored for flavor. An oval gilt mirror
will curl you about like a gray cat in a Steuben bowl
who is untroubled by the union of sight and smell or

the impossibility of wholeness. In rare cases, presenting
congruent reflections, mirrors invert and they will
reverse only on the vertical medial axis. Your right hand is
the left hand of the reflection of you reaching but failing again:

the Kentucky Homecoming Queen who was not crowned,
stretching for the rhinestones, the roses, always straining
to hear your name blaring from stadium speakers so
your mother in the stands will hear. Could a mirror be

your guide as you reach back to touch your mother the night
she came to your game? Summer, playing softball under
the lights, running from the smell of sewage, you caught
your breath like a grounder when she sat down in the front

bleachers. No. The mirror can't help you find what did not
happen. Unity and completion are other desires mirrors can't
fill, only prove the impossibility of feeling the sting
of your mother's knees bleeding from carpet burn as

she climbed risers, one by one, to wipe dust from backs
and corners. Your poems, like fragments in a mirror's
shard, substitute words for reality like your mother who left
lights on in the coop to fool nesting hens into behaving like

it was day. Mirrors will not interpret or correlate internal
and external self, can't be interpreted like a metaphor. What is
withheld is not there. Unlike helium that seeps from birthday
balloons, the praise, the love your mother did not give

you, was not in her. If, while reading what you'd written
to your mother, your pen rolled onto the floor, she would
have leaned without grunting, to pick it up and put it smack dab
in the kitchen table's center, not where you'd left it on the edge.

03-14-28

This snow is what I pray death will be.
I am released from myself, from guilt,
from driving across Whitney Lakes to visit
my mother in her nursing home. I can excuse
myself as easily as I do from a table. Moved
with my father, his cancer, from Kentucky
to Connecticut, my mother gave her past,
her present, her future to me. If I don't visit

her here in this Yankee state, no one will.
Instead of memories, the lima bean I lodged
in my ear, she keeps a list: emery board, Ponds.
My mother does not search for a way out, press
the code, 03-14-28, to open locks as I do
each day, every day when I lug her to my home
to visit my father imprisoned by his ribs, black
lines on a bone scan. Their fifty-eight year

marriage is forgotten, like a hotel she checked
out of last July. My mother's path is circular
in Memory Care: wellness station, hairdresser,
back again. Always lost, slippered feet shuffle,
keeping pace with her walker, patent purse
elbowed into her side. I admire packets
of Kleenex she won at Bingo the night before,
how she threads marbles of glass. Unstrung

by the recreation therapist each evening,
each morning is a resurrection for my mother.
Wearing her bead necklace I finger into a rosary
of worries, I wonder if like my golden retriever,
my mother can make a decision, get up, stretch

as my dog does from the rug, think *bed*. If I hold
out our communion of beaten biscuit and ham
trayed on my palm, will she remember the taste?

Mother's Day Brunch at Whitney Manor

I recite phrases I've learned to cope with Alzheimer's,
to get through Belgian waffles and the carving station:
lights are on, but—; the elevator doesn't go to top floors;
soft as a grape or melon I fork from the salad station.

Still hoping to impress Mother, I choose several slices
of exotic melons that have appeared this year like
orange-fleshed Cavaillon, native to the south of France,
or the evergreen-pink flesh of European Piel del Sapo.

I predict canary yellow Amarelo tastes like pineapple.
Galia will be Southeast Asian spice. Persian or Spanish
melons have a borderline personality like my mother.
Shake, thump, incant spells over the dome, these melons

remain implacable, endlessly perverse, Mother's rival
in disguises. Secretive, self-contained, migrating field
to field, exteriors change. Go to last summer's fruit stand
— no pale green watermelons in the shape of a football,

but dark green soccer balls with chartreuse pin stripes.
The cantaloupe, for example, is imperturbable, its netting
growing looser or denser, depending upon point of origin.
Like a parrot, the Crenshaw will have molted from lime

to a light yellow. I know that perfect melons have *innies*
for bellybuttons, for a ripe one, I need to sniff umbilical
wounds sustained separating from stems, that I must stop
inhaling Mother's Chantilly bath powder, awakening

my childhood, or abandon yearning to be a full slip melon,
so heavy it falls from the natal vine. But today, a gymnast,

I grab, celebrate what we have left of our Mother's Day,
this world, before flesh changes to mealy mush in my hand.

No Apogee

The wait for dawn over, a heron is pulled into flight, a word
like Alzheimer's that I do not understand. In Morgan Point's
cove, oval stones are washed by tide, helpless as I am pulled

by habit, by love. Long Island Sound is corrugated. There is
no way for water to resist wind, or for me to keep from dialing
my mother every morning in her bee hive of white heads.

No apogee. Nothing changes except position of her recliner.
Watching her future contract, I know she is no work in progress.
Moved to North Carolina near my sister, my mother does

not phone me in Connecticut. Long distance charges still mean
something to her. Hearts of Queen Anne's lace have taught
me how blood knots, why I call, start each day with hearing

she cannot hear, see, walk, how eggs are always scrambled
and the toast cold. Each day she remembers less and less.
My evenings close by learning she's gotten through one more

day, what I should have chiseled on her gravestone. I reply,
Each day will come and go, but not again. My words never
stay. Each night, I repeat: *Eat Florida cantaloupe, have*

a Georgia peach while they are in season. I send horehound
drops to soothe a cough, to show her a taste of the past can
bring pleasure. When I visit, I promise we'll fill a bucket

with blackberries, bake a cobbler. No Tennyson, I can't create
a Ulysses who will seek and find the world again. Of motion,
she knows less and less, but there is grammar, a geometry

in her course: her walker circles on her circles and hours
in the atrium are punctuated by meals. September 11, 2001.
She watches twin towers of the World Trade Center collapse.

Be grateful, I say, that you never lost a child, but my mother
thinks only of what's been taken from her. She does not
understand DNA, does not care that families will not have

even a body to mourn as she did when we buried my father
in Kentucky. I cannot undo my mother's corset of memories.
Newly young, a widower who joins her table for breakfast

will not pluck an April day from her. Lips sealed to song,
she has nothing left to say of my first steps. I want to move
through my mother again. Without her I will be an orphan.

Am I afraid to say goodbye each night because I may say
goodbye to myself, from the breath I drew from her heart?
The heron stalks, spears. It is the hour for eels, the hour

for me to call. Like a cricket I cannot find, unsettling me
by lifting wings with its shiver of off rhythm, thoughts
of my mother will madden me if I cannot let her world be.

Dust Rag

bound/ by countless silken ties
of love and thought
    —Robert Frost

Finally, I don't need to lie about being lazy
by saying I do not not swipe ceiling corners
so the cobwebs can veil the moon. I even
finger dirt on my picture frames, write
my name on table tops, blow a cloud

from the fireplace's mantle. My mother
would wipe not write about dust, not sit
at the kitchen counter as I do, light like
my tarnished pewter, or lead of a pencil
before erasure. My mother punctuated

all her days, ending in a period or question
of what had she done to suffer so. There
were no exclamation points. When she
took my sister and me to the town beach,
she'd tie one end of a rope to each of us

and the other end to her leg so we could
go in the water while she sat on shore.
Surely, she must have had stories she kept
curled under clenched knuckles white as
snow or flour. I don't remember my mother

playing hide and seek. She was too busy
ironing, hemming and frying chicken.
The click of my jaw was almost audible
when on her final visit, she bottom scooted
on my floor to clean the baseboards, used

cleanser on the bathtub I'd gotten in to scrub
before she'd even stand up in it to shower—
no soaking in my tub for her. I was her first born:
Lloyd High's yearbook editor, Valedictorian,
U.K.'s Homecoming Queen—it was her due.

There never was any question between us of
who was the sun, who was the earth. Ripped
in half, paper I throw in the corner is big as
rags she used to tear in strips to quilt. Why
am I still threading her veins through my text?

In Separateness Only
Does Love Learn Definition

—Robert Penn Warren

We stand at the bus stop. Eyeing my son and me,
the other children are quiet and they look hard.
It's not their first day of class. My fingers tighten as if

curled in my father's hand at six years: cowbarn, outhouse,
cornbread, woodpile, chickenhouse. He rode a plowhorse
named Snip, no big yellow bus. A greyhound, Queenie,

uncurled from under a forsythia bush outside the kitchen,
leaping to race him, but my grandmother held her collar.
Before Daddy rode off, Grandpa told him about the last wild

horses in Kentucky. Scoured out of hills, they were roped,
tied down, nostrils clamped shut. Their neck veins pulsed
like salmon jumping upstream. The mares all aborted.

I know beyond that word. Hanging limp as morning
wet grass, my son's hands are smooth not toughened from
milking a cow as my father's were by the time he went

to first grade. I want to double fence a pasture to protect
him like Daddy did to keep stallions apart in order
to keep them spirited for breeding. Eric waits, but strains

to see beyond the corner. I pull him back, fearing roads
I cannot see him travel. The day must come when I will force
his snowsuited body out, without immunity, into January

mornings so cold milk jugs would freeze if I left them out
on the doorstep. Can I be ready with a message to pin on him
as his boots scale snow, tracking maps I have not traced?

Boarding the bus, Eric twists around to me from the landing
and I reach out to touch his shoulder, then stand waving him
out of sight. My stomach cupped in my hands, I bow my head

and let my son go. Knowing how wild horses are broken,
I pray to him: remember the soles of your bare feet running
through bluegrass blooming over hills in Hardin County.

GRABBLING FOR CATFISH
IN CUMBERLAND LAKE, KENTUCKY

My son Todd and I were stuck on shore. I had returned
the rowboat the night before, even though neither of us
caught a fish. He blamed me for my inexperience, for being
born a woman, for not being his father who'd know tricks

like spitting on a worm before throwing it in, and how to bait
hooks with dough balls or offal. It was useless to explain
half a day's rental costs almost as much as a full one and
a support check from his father hadn't come for two months.

My son could scatter blame like blowing heads off dandelions.
Limestone ridges make it easy to forget the day Wolf Creek Dam
was opened. The lodge photo showed a man in a green park shirt
releasing the gate and turning sky loose. Foaming at the mouth,

water swallowed the valley whole. It was spring. Under the dark
of the lake's skin, catfish were holed up to spawn in roots
for cover. I decided, time to teach my son about grabbling,
show him I was not afraid of reaching down into the unknown,

let a catfish grab my hand and hold on for dear life. I found
a stump, settled down, plunged in. I'd learned from my uncle
not to short arm. Explaining grabbling was also called noodling,
I described wiggling my fingers like wet spaghetti, rippling

my wrist like cooked lasagna. No catfish could resist! Knotting
a rope to a nail for a stringer to run through gills, I lifted whiskers,
blue skin. Way too small for such a big hole, Todd got to take
it home alive in a bucket. I shaded our trophy by the side door

under canvas from a deck chair, but Saturday morning, getting ready
for the dump, I broom handled the body. No rot, no odor,

no wound. To ease my son's guilt over his promise to keep
the fish alive, I could've described death in Cumberland Lake:

grinning mouth that would eat anything was a home for leeches;
mites in pits of lidless eyes; intestines bleached to rubber bands,
swaying with green and bronze flies. Afraid Todd would not
sleep at night, instead I fielded questions about the catfish's soul.

Would flying be like swimming? I resisted saying what's awkward
in air, like passion, has grace in water, but grace can disappear
like his father's desire for me. What's gone was gone—our family,
and elms rotting at the base of Wolf Dam, stripped limbs rising

as if lifting to heaven. Wanting Todd to remember me as daring,
I told him to picture the catfish big as a man in the lodge's photo
that might have been lurking where I went grabbling. I will
not forget realizing I could be brave, overcome the thought

of snapping turtles, water moccasins. This was the day I learned
I could float without thinking of the drowned valley beneath me,
the shards of lives like mine archaeologists would never unearth.
Spelling each other, Todd and I rowed an hour to find an inlet to

drop anchor near folds of limestone and chimneys of crayfish. I
was grateful for water more accessible than creeks in Harlan County
hollows so Todd could see when one shore closed, the lake began
to open another one, hinting at another one beyond every bend.

AGAINST THAT NIGHT

A bitter edge has been added today. As a small boy,
never wanting to say good night to me, Eric fought
off going to sleep, belly laughing like Savin Rock's

lady in the glass case rocking in her orange and red
flowered dress. I was sure where fact and fiction met,
like hands pressed to a mirror, until confirmation class

became a dance my son did around Sunday morning
authority, until I got the church's call asking why he
had dropped out. Cupping car keys, nothing I can

mouth about speed, alcohol, Scott who died last fall
at sixteen will inflate a raft to keep him afloat. Lifting
slats of the blind, I watch him back out the drive. I am

left with memory of sweeping blacktop to clear worms
lured by promise in spring rain. Like juggling snowballs
after they melt, Eric's face stays with me. My son knows

how to head soccer balls, but not the thrust of a tongue.
When some girl touches him, he will not think of my love,
my hands peeling potatoes. Will he shiver, shake off

water like our golden retriever does after climbing out
of High Lane Pond? Pulled from sleep, I wait, then
palm walls of the hall to Eric's room. Reaching out for

the light switch, I stop. A voice I do not recognize comes
from his bedroom and stubs the dark. Will he tell me if
the girl's hands pulled him down? Knowing just what

a mother can't ask her son, what he won't answer, I jerk
questions back. Edging corners, I crabwalk to bed, stalked
by her whisper shrilling like wings of swans in the night.

THE STEP-FATHER READS *THE SNOW QUEEN*

Teaching Matthew to read in second grade
tempted me to revise Webster's Dictionary, erase
step from *father* in his vocabulary. Our favorite
author was Hans Christian Andersen. Matthew

chose *The Snow Queen* every day of our first winter
together, comparing the holly tree we'd planted
to mark the day his mother and I married and we
became a family to a bush of red berries half buried

by snow where the reindeer put Gerda down
in her glacial search for her brother, Kai, who had
been enchanted by the Snow Queen. Afternoons
when Matthew came straight home, I knew he had

failed again to recognize words reading out loud
in *Take a Turn*. When it was my step-son's night
to carry a poster to read at the PTA book fair,
we flipped to the pages about Gerda who carried

words on a dried fish written by a Lapland woman
to an old Finland woman who learned them by heart
so she could eat the cod in porridge. Wanting Matthew
to read not memorize his poster, I'd drum my fingers,

rotate letters like parts of a Chinese puzzle, so he
could place index cards around syllables, frozen
for him like the 100 pieces of almost identical ice
that the Snow Queen used to trap Kai on her lake.

Hands numbed, Kai shaped out whole sentences
with ice, unable each time to fit edges together

that spelled the key to undoing the queen's spell.
Won over by Gerda's love for her brother, Kai,

shards of ice fell and formed the magic word, the one
I hoped to engrave on a stone with Matthew: *Eternity.*
Letters in *Eternity* freed Kai from the Snow Queen,
but no Hans Christian Andersen, the alphabet was one

strange shape after another for Matthew. At seven,
he still touched each letter, lost in lines that looped
like a maze with the exits blocked by long and short
vowels. Guessing at most words, Matthew wrestled

then clacked consonants on his tongue. Though small
in number, *A, E, I, O, U* were a regiment blocking
progress by constantly shifting battle formations
like flakes did sent from the Snow Queen to attack

Gerda as she struggled to find her brother, Kai.
Even with *step* in my vocabulary, like Gerda, I refused
to give up, wouldn't paste labels *learning disabled*
or *dyslexic* on Matthew. Unable to sound out phonic

combinations, he slowly started to recognize letters
in a pattern, whispering in my ear so his mother
would not hear him and take a shower to muffle
her sorrow at his failure to read. Like hopping rocks

in a creek, my son would finger words he could
pronounce and if he stumbled, he knew he could
turn to me. After two months, Matthew crossed
a whole line without stammering. At China Inn

on his eighth birthday, he was not afraid to crack
a fortune cookie. For me, red letters on a paper strip

he read rose up just as the enchanted ice pieces did for Kai who freed by Gerda's tears, danced for joy.

THE STEP-FATHER SPEAKS

I. Botany Lesson for Shakespeare

On our first vacation after becoming a family,
Matthew, his mother and I drove from Connecticut
to California. Unable to read road signs, the son
I had acquired like a dowry made up a game for us

out of spotting the Jerusalem Artichoke that laced
highways in every state. Debating whether to label
the sunflowers golden, orange, or yellow, the first
one of us to spot their big heads when we came

to a border got two dollars to spend at the next rest
stop. Showing Matthew why he should read, I opened,
Audubon's *Guide to North American Wildflowers*.
The Jerusalem Artichoke was planted by Indians

then spread eastward. In 1805, Lewis and Clark
dined on the tubers baked by a squaw in territory
later labeled North Dakota. In his diary, Clark
recorded the Jerusalem Artichoke with its potato

texture and sweet, nut taste. The common name
for the flower was corrupted from the Italian *girasole*:
turning to the sun. Black, its eyes were like holes
in an untanned leather belt, a reminder to me that

what states had in common bound them together,
not the name of a country. My heart kept troping
toward my new son, but I was unable to stem
the yearning to reseed. I did have an answer for

Romeo to Juliet's question, *What's in a name?* On
Matthew, my last name could dovetail our ragged
family border like *girasole* crossing all boundaries,
east to west, naturally cohering one coast to another.

II. Night Fishing at Morgan Point

Weighted down by frozen bait, insurance
that my son and I would never need lures,
we were linked by ritual of hook and rod.

Matthew had dipped into schools of kellies;
to show him how to secure one, keep it alive
by pushing steel through middle, I pictured

the blue heron his brother had nicknamed
Doctor Doom for the deadly aim of its bill.
Cradling his hands, I wanted to tell him how

I held him on the ride home just a day
after he was born, how his mother and I
drank champagne, making love on the sand

at Morgan Point the night he was conceived,
how I packed her suitcase before rushing her
to the hospital, filling her room with roses,

how I watched his head emerge. None of this
happened. No priest consecrating bread
and wine to place the Eucharist in outstretched

hands and tongues, I could not perform
a sacrament transfusing my love into his blood.
Our talk was of stars, not my fear that Matthew

might become inscrutable to me. With nothing to
say, I'd have a beer before settling down to wait
the arcing of the line flung out over the moon.

Lashing at the dark, we would cast into unfamiliar
depths. A shining whipped the night, hung like
a shred, before my son reeled in the first snapper.

I did teach him that he must gut fish he catches
so they do not rot, and I showed him how to hold
a knife while he cut the fillets for us to grill. Later,

beginning our own tradition, we fed one another
the first bite from the striped bass we'd caught,
from the meal we had created, from flesh we shared.

III. Driving Lesson

Knuckles whiter than a wedding tent on the burl knob
of the stick shift, we jerk pulling away from
the light. *Hey Dad, chill out. It can't be worse than me*

riding a Harley, my son shouts over Rolling Stones'
latest CD. At least we have their music,
one thing in common, not like our last names that

will never be the same on a license. I did not create
his life, and I wonder now at what I am doing
flipping keys, letting him steer. Lurching forward

when my son accelerates, I hold onto the word *Dad*,
grip the handle above the window, remind
myself of the latest TV commercials, Volvo's safety

record. At least, he is still staying between the lines,
not leaving ruts in the median, and knows
that he does not have a right of way to turn left into

the intersection. Matthew's unsure of when to brake.
I can't suppress *Stop;* he never stifles *Fuck.*
Slowing down on Evergreen, we see the tree that ended

Scott McNeill. Dead four years, Chris is alive, paralyzed
from his neck down and the girl driving the VW
just graduated from Brown. Memorial stripes of yellow,

red, green bleed into the oak. No one comes to sing
Scott's song, Bob Marley's *One Love;* no one visits
Chris. Rain coats asphalt; our car hydroplanes and drifts

to the left lane. We look at each other, both afraid of wheels
sliding by themselves and for his life, for another Scott,
another Chris he will control after I step away from the car.

IV. The Step-father Becomes the Father

Do years add layers as silt does, filtering down through a river,
flowing quietly, sure of its direction as we have been for ten

years? There was no ritual for becoming a family when I married
your mother. Our three last names stayed separate, were not

blended into one word we could stencil on a mailbox. I did not
understand your mother's anger at years she could not erase.

She removed monograms from silver but couldn't change your
last name to hers. At times, her rage was a fire, scorching all

175

earth around us. Peace, like dandelions we dug year after year,
jagged spears of green spreading out to yellow carpets, crept in,

pushing back the blackness farther and farther. One day it was
faint, a ring surrounding us, and then it was memory. Because it

is easy, the metaphor of planting comes readily. So common, but
I can't think of another comparison that would not be contrived,

that would be natural for a step-father's love that is not. What
I did not seed, I can harvest; the earth has been deeded to me.

Yet, as I stand at Sachem Field waiting behind the soccer posts,
I sometimes fall silent, not screaming out *Yes!* as other fathers do

when their sons score a goal. Another man's name broadcast
over the P.A. system slaps my ears. At the fall sports banquet,

after being picked All Conference and MVP, you called me up
to the podium. While we stood posing for the *North Haven Post*,

need to see my name engraved on you for a plaque I'd mount
in the hall fell from my heart. With no words in our vocabulary

for *blood, own,* or *real,* we each grasped a handle; there was no
step or hyphen labeling love bridging us, the trophy we shared.

If I Could Choose: A, B, C, D, None of the Above

Waiting out chemotherapy, I'll pencil in by evaporation at 101
    like my grandmother, pick a final breath that doesn't
arouse me from sleep or one that surprises me right in

the middle of stripping an artichoke. I refuse to lie here, to worry
    if I will live through autumn or even last out September,
this rain. I thought I'd felt every lump, come full circle.

Ed, the ends unravel with your love. You tell me to picture
    myself standing, head bared, hanging out of a third class
train window while I plunge through northern Italy.

I invent a history for us, watch it unwind on tracks, imagine
    three boys we might have conceived, trading cards as
they negotiate: Whitey Ford, Babe Ruth, Sammy Sosa,

Mickey Mantle, Mark McGwire. Toeing limestone, we would've
    carried our sons' cleats, smelled mowed grass, heard crickets
a cappella. When you finally could repeat *cancer*,

I told you about steering with one finger in my yellow Porsche
    at 140, hoping to tempt concrete so my mother wouldn't ask,
Where did I fail her? The tumor in my head was not

sharp or bright, but was hidden like the diamond you took from
    your father's Masonic ring that I wear on a chain. When I
draped my head to hide the scar, I was sure you'd leave,

but you spoke of deserts you'd explored: Sahara, Namib, Rub'al
    Khali, Aracama, Talla Makan. Recalling wild berries in Mojave,
sweet on stripped branches, you compared me to paper

flowers in the Sonora, hair like petals, thin but persistent. A lizard
    of Chihuahua, shriveled by sun, I would wait for October, not
be a cereus, drab by day, with a white bloom bursting once to

roman candle July. Afraid, I watch out windows for you to walk up
    Autumn Street. Skylights frame the black, a backdrop for
stars. I cannot stop imagining my death might be opening

a door and smiling like you always do. No promise has been given.
    Positioning me by the birch, you split, then pile wood, to let
winter know we're ready with gloves unpacked.

The Difference Between a Raw Onion and a Slow-Cooked One

I strip to skin hidden during the day, allow
sagging underarms I keep hidden in sleeves

to wobble. I'm counting on the moon not to
cut through clouds, dilute the ink black cove

blotting years annotated by stretch marks. I
I can't stop myself from timing waves lapping,

imposing patterns, making rules for the ocean
like aging I also can't control. Habits of love have

turned you into a fish in Mammoth Cave that has
no eyes. Calling out, you tell me to sit right up

on pink Stony Creek granite in front of neighbors,
let high tide lick my feet, smooth off my edges.

A cook like Molly O'Neill, you'll teach me
how to enjoy hammock time by eating summer

food that breaks down walls, changes internal
sugars. Cooking this late in August, we need

to layer flavors and textures of thirty-eight years
we have spent together, learn to mix the fierce

with the mellow. You finger my spine, perhaps
trying to figure how I am connected, but I imagine

you as a vegetable chef breaking peapods open
at the vein, clean every time. No vegan, it does

not comfort me to hear raw carrots or peppers,
with cell walls firm as adolescent buttocks,

restrict the release of sweet tasting compounds,
or that baked, garlic sags as it loses its fire,

but gains a touch of soul. Without something
aggressive and dark below the surface, sweetness,

like youth, becomes cloying, is more fleeting
than lasting. Knowing I am afraid to reshape what

has cooled, with your thumb hooked on my wrist,
you lecture about chemical reactions: rearranged,

proteins can evaporate bitter tasting compounds.
Generated by a convection oven, or by emotion,

heat like passion changes everything, is able to
melt solids to liquid, even within the human heart.

For My Husband at Eighty

A spade dangles in your hand when you talk but with no faith in spring, you do not have the heart to work cold ground. Summer's not a sure thing and you won't plant lilium bulbs you might not see burst to bloom. Even the most casual remark can cause you to bristle. On our afternoon drives to Essex, I point out choke cherry seeds buried into igneous crevices. You predict they will sprout only to be felled by saws of Connecticut road crews. There's no topic I can broach: a gull that begs for scraps of shrimp outside Jimmy's in West Haven brushes our windshield, then lands on the hood, spreading out its wings to shroud us like a sheet will do.

For god's sake! Wait until May. Plant petunias, rows and rows of marigolds or line the stone walls with zinnias we can cut. Walk out in early morning, come back around dusk and each purple, orange, white and yellow will still be there, safe and tame, a sure thing. With no spirit to hold them though the winter, blossoms and stems will be turned over into a compost.

Eat with your head down. It's been years since you went to work, claimed a parking spot with your name. Now you stay at home. You don't believe in immortality so you won't plant sage or, for that matter, mint for wisdom and thyme for bravery. It's sure too late for lavender's purity and virtue. No rosemary, there is too much to remember: dressed for Halloween, your mother in the pink dotted swiss your father in the purple flowered dress, before stomach cancer caused him to beg you to release him. Still young, your sister still alive, pouting in your father's Buick, staying the rebel even dying on St. Patrick's Day from starvation rather than live chained by Multiple Sclerosis.

Maybe I should plant statice and globe amaranth to give you eternal light. Getting lost in shadowed rooms cluttered like a library full of Hume and Joyce you'll never read again, you finger what you have not done, the Philip Morris stock you sold to come to Yale, the son and daughter you did not raise. Wild seeds you sowed year after year were no metaphor: riding your Harley over Maine hills with Hank, threatening to jump from the balcony of Long Wharf Theater with Michael, being tossed out of every bar after the Harvard-Yale game in Boston, the trips from Rudy's Bar to Archie Moore's, then back again. Hands on the wheel at three o'clock in the morning, straightening out Missouri curves for speed, as if on roller blades, you crossed over yellow lines, singing *Baby, I was born to run.* That was right before you shattered your hip, the left one that gives you so much trouble at night or if you bend to pull off boots.

Here in Connecticut with New England cold that can stretch out through half a year, October to late March, there's a beauty in withered weeks that withstand snow and ice. What can't be seen mixed into summer's foliage, steps to center stage in winter. Life-everlasting, goldenrod, pinweed and wild grass are far more interesting in February than in late July when their beauty is overshadowed by Casa Blanca lilies and the plumes of astilbe. What endures has new strength that can be put to different use. Mulleins, cotton-grass, cattails, johns-wort, meadowsweet, hardhack and other strong stemmed plants not snapped by long cold provide granaries for cardinals that want to feed in February.

Poised spearing a julep, mint smells good in summer but it has odor you can savor in winter, too. The mint family has names you might not know: spearmint, peppermint, basil, rosemary, sage, thyme, oregano, lavender, hyssop, horehound and catnip as well as the bright red garden flower, salvia.

Hard to distinguish during summer, in winter the square stem and opposite branches are clear. When the flower petals are dried and gone, long and tubular, the toothed calyx shrivels and remains with four nutlets. Dry and wrinkled like you, they are still a treat for yellow finches.

You'll never be hot pink phlox shedding moldy leaves or an iris whose upright fans can be sheared and reset. Let me compare you to wild yams that blend in with their surroundings in summer, but in winter, anyone with an eye for form can't help but notice three-sided hearts twining in among dried stalks of annuals like geraniums that were red but now are just bleached bones without the passion or wildness needed to carry them through the killing frost.

OLD HORSES

This moon's for horses
that cannot sleep past three
in the morning. We have seen
them on October nights
gathering autumn. Old horses.
Sudden, the flare of their eyes,
matches in the dark,
as if reflecting the full face
of the moon were enough for joy.
Their heads streaming down, parted
darkness as your hands in my wet
hair did. How it fell to waves under
your comb. I leaned into you
while tortoise teeth dripped brown
like oars pulling bottom weeds,
shining deep as the auburn of our first
summer. Now weighted by shadow,
you finger free my hair at dusk,
then unbridle our strawberry roan,
letting her run into the last light.

About the Author

Connecticut State University Distinguished Professor, Vivian Shipley teaches at Southern Connecticut State University where she was named Faculty Scholar in 2000, 2005 and 2008. Her eleventh book, *Perennial*, was published in 2015 by Negative Capability Press and was nominated for the Pulitzer Prize and named the Paterson Poetry Prize Finalist. *The Poet*, her tenth book, was published in 2015 by *Louisiana Literature* Press, Southeastern Louisiana University. *All of Your Messages Have Been Erased* (*Louisiana Literature* Press, SLU, 2010) was nominated for the Pulitzer Prize, won the Sheila Motton Book Prize from the New England Poetry Club, the Paterson Award for Sustained Literary Achievement and the CT Press Club Award for Best Creative Writing. Her sixth chapbook is *Greatest Hits: 1974-2010* (Pudding House Press, Youngstown, Ohio, 2010). She has received the Library of Congress's Connecticut Lifetime Achievement Award for Service to the Literary Community and a Connecticut Book Award for Poetry two times. Most recently, she won the 2017-18 Steve Kowit Prize for Poetry for "Cargo" from San Diego Arts & Entertainment Guild. In 2015, she won the Hackney Literary Award for Poetry for "Foxfire." Other poetry awards for individual poems include the Lucille Medwick Prize from the Poetry Society of America, the Robert Frost Foundation Poetry Prize, the Ann Stanford Poetry Prize from the University of Southern California, the Marble Faun Poetry Prize from the William Faulkner Society, the Daniel Varoujan Prize from the New England Poetry Club and the Hart Crane Prize from Kent State. Raised in Kentucky, a member of the University of Kentucky Hall of Distinguished Alumni, the highest award the university can bestow on an alumnus, she has a PhD from Vanderbilt University and lives in North Haven, Connecticut with her husband, Ed Harris.